D1408179

EVERYDAY INVENTIONS

MEREDITH HOOPER

TAPLINGER PUBLISHING COMPANY
NEW YORK

Illustrated and designed by Graham Wade

Grateful acknowledgment for photographs is made to:

Radio Times Hulton Picture Library: pp. 5 (top), 21, 26-7, 49, 57, 60 (left), 68, 70-1, 74, 99, 121; Science Museum, London: pp. 2, 4, 5 (bottom), 7, 9, 17, 61 (left), 76, 77 (right), 91-2, 116, 125, 128-9, 131; Rubber And Plastics Research Association of Great Britain: pp. 28-9, 30 (bottom left), 31-2, 35-6, 37 (from One Hundred Years Of Vulcanized Rubber — American Chemical Society); United States Library of Congress: pp. 19, 23-4, 66, 86-9, 115, 118; Victoria and Albert Museum, London: pp. 10-15, 135; Kellogg Company: pp. 108-9, 111, 113; Tin Research Institute: pp. 83-4; Otis Elevator Company: pp. 61 (right), 63; Coca Cola Company: pp.105, 107; Yale Locks: pp. 12-13; Australian News And Information Bureau: pp. 45, 50; Food and Agricultural Organization: p. 59; United States Information Service: p. 60; British Museum: p. 40; Natural Rubber Producers Research Association, Great Britain: p. 30 (bottom right); National Milk Publicity Council, Incorporated: p. 81; Unigate Ltd: p. 80; Butterick Archives: p. 121 (right); Art-Wood Photography, London: p. 127; Central Photographic Unit, Fort Dunlop: p. 38; The New South Wales Department of Tourist Activities: p. 67; Routledge and Kegan Paul: p. 20 (advertisement in Strange Story of False Teeth — John Woodforde); I.B.M. Ltd: p. 133; Gillette Industries Ltd: p. 42; The Hoover Company: p. 78.

First published in the United States in 1976 by
TAPLINGER PUBLISHING CO., INC.
New York, New York

Library of Congress Catalog Card Number: 76–5624
ISBN 0–8008–2544–6

CONTENTS

THE WHEELBARROW

Wooden Ox and Gliding Horse

Europeans have been using the wheelbarrow for about eight hundred years. But the Chinese invented it at least ten centuries before that. Ancient Chinese gave wheelbarrows nice names—Wooden Ox and Gliding Horse. "In the time taken by a man (with a similar burden) to go six feet, the Wooden Ox would go twenty feet," wrote an admiring historian in A.D. 430. "It could carry the food supply (of one man) for a whole year, and yet after twenty miles the porter would not feel tired."

A famous general called Chuko Liang developed wheelbarrows two hundred years before this historian was writing, to help carry supplies for his army. But, very recently, pictures have been discovered on ancient tombs, and bricks, of even earlier wheelbarrows. So perhaps they were invented in the first century A.D.

No one knows how people in Europe found out about the wheelbarrow—or, for that matter, about many other Chinese inventions. Perhaps the idea came overland across the steppes, with nomadic tribes. Or perhaps traders using the famous silk-route to the great city of Constantinople, on the eastern edge of the Mediterranean, talked about things seen in far-off China. Probably someone who heard the talk worked out his own version, because the wheelbarrow used

in Europe is a different design from the Chinese. It has the wheel out in front, so that the load is supported both by the wheel and the man pushing it. The wheelbarrow in China has the wheel in the middle, right under the load, and the pusher only has to steer and balance it. At all events, sometime in the twelfth or thirteenth century, workmen building the great castles and cathedrals of Europe had, to their great relief, a new, simple device to help them. One man with a wheelbarrow could carry the same load as two men and much more easily and quickly. The wheel took the place of a man.

In China the wheelbarrow was used to transport people as well as loads, and it does still. Up to six passengers could fit on one big version, pulled by a mule or donkey and guided from behind by a driver. On another type, the traveller sat one side of the large wheel and his luggage balanced him on the other. Early European visitors were very impressed. "The sight of this wheelbarrow thus loaded was entirely new to me," wrote a Dutch visitor. "I even think that in many cases such a barrow would be found much superior to ours." There were even wheelbarrows in China fitted with sails, like a junk, so that the wind could help to push them. Tales of sailing wheelbarrows really did fascinate men in far-off Europe!

Medieval wheelbarrows

NAILS

Men have been using nails for the last five and a half thousand years

Someone—no one knows who for certain—invented an entirely new way of building wooden houses in 1833. Traditionally, heavy wooden beams, one-foot-thick, were fitted together to form the solid framework for a house. Corners were made by sharpening the end of one beam and fitting it into an accurately cut hole in the next beam. For extra strength a wooden peg could be driven through both. All this took many days' work by skilled carpenters. But in 1833, in Chicago, there weren't enough carpenters to go around and too many people wanted somewhere to live in a hurry. Chicago grew from being a frontier trading-post to the fourth largest city in the world, all in a hundred years. The new type of house which appeared in Chicago had a skeleton made of thin sawn lengths of wood, *nailed* together. The basic idea is so simple, and so much used today all over the world, that it is hard to realize it ever had to be invented. It was like a big, light basket: all the different pieces of wood took the strain together. Critics said the first strong wind would blow it down and called it the "balloon-frame house". But three-quarters of all houses in the United States are built this way today. It took about a week to put the balloon-frame house up, and just about anyone who could use a hammer and nails could do the job.

Noah building the Ark

Coment une ceig commence a noel faire une arche et y mettre une paire de toutes bestes pour le deluge:

Men have been using nails for the last five and a half thousand years. But right up until the nineteenth century, nails were made by hand. It was a slow job, and nails were things to be treated with respect. The balloon-frame house would have been impossible without the invention, at the beginning of the nineteenth century in America, of machinery to mass-produce nails cheaply. The first machines stamped out nails from flat sheets of metal. In later years they were cut and shaped from wire. Nails could now be dropped, wasted, bent, banged into wood with gay abandon—all the things we are used to doing—because there was an unending supply.

Blacksmith in 15th century

In medieval times a nail-maker forged iron into rough bars, then hammered pieces through a graded series of holes till he had made the right shape, and finally flattened a lump at one end to make the head. Nails of copper, brass or iron were used for putting floorboards together, roofs on buildings, locks on chests, leather coverings on chairs, hinges on doors, copper bottoms on ships, shoes on horses.

Roman nails

In 1606 an Englishman, Sir Bevis Bulmer, patented probably the first machine to help with nail-making. It was not very successful, but it did cut the iron into rods of various thicknesses.

American machines were introduced into England in the nineteenth century. But in 1830 in England there were at least sixty thousand men, women and children who earned their living from hand-making nails. They worked at home. At the beginning of the week the nail master handed out nail iron which was already slit into rods of various sizes. At the end of the week the workers turned in a pile of hand-forged nails. It was hard, poorly paid work. Slowly the machinery took over and began to produce nails by the ton, not the pound. But there were still some hand nail-makers working in England at the beginning of this century, producing nails little different in appearance from those the Romans made two thousand years ago.

"Of all the results of human ingenuity, there is nothing more simple, more generally useful, or more efficient in its universal application, than a nail."

THE YARD AND THE METRE

How many of us have a foot a foot long?

A yard is roughly the distance between the end of your nose and the tip of your index finger, arm outstretched. But every human being's body is not the same size. How many of us have a foot a foot long? So King Henry I of England declared that a yard was the exact distance between the tip of *his* nose and the tip of *his* outstretched index finger, and wrote this definition into the statute books. At least that is the traditional story. Probably chiefs and kings had been saying for hundreds of years that a yard was the length between *their* noses and fingers. All measurements started off in a casual way such as this, and most of them were related to parts of the human body. An inch, for example, was originally a thumb's breadth. A yard is actually twice the length of a cubit—an ancient and widely used measurement often mentioned in the Bible. The cubit was the distance between the tip of the index finger and the point of the elbow.

Measurements (and weights) needed to be standardized if they were to be of any real use. This meant making a standard unit out of something lasting, like metal or stone, and keeping it in a safe and obvious place for reference. Ancient Egyptians kept their units of measurement in the temples. In many European cities the standard unit of measurement dating back to medieval times can still be seen in a public place such as the outer wall of the cathedral, in the main square. But any system of weights and measures is always being made more precise; factors such as changing temperatures, the type of materials used, and where the standard is kept, all affect its accuracy. When the British Houses of Parliament burnt down in 1834, the standard yard and the standard pound weight were destroyed, so new ones had to be made. In 1878 the British Imperial Yard was defined by law as the distance at 62° Fahrenheit between two fine lines engraved on gold studs sunk into a particular bronze bar.

During the French Revolution, at the end of the eighteenth century, Frenchmen were keen to reorganize their lives. The French system of weights and measures was most unsatisfactory, inherited like everyone else's from the past. In 1790 the French government decided to bring in a new system, using logical, easy-to-handle decimals. The new unit of length was to be the metre; it would be one ten-millionth of the meridional distance from the North Pole to the Equator, measured through Paris. This gave a

The yard in the time of Henry I of England

length fairly close to the existing French measurement, as well as to the Italian and the English.

Scientists were directed to work out the exact distance between Dunkirk, on the coast of France, and Barcelona, in Spain, from which the length of the metre could be calculated. But the calculations turned out to be much more difficult than anyone anticipated. In 1795, before the work was finished, the government decided to go ahead anyway and adopt the metric system. Four years later, the standard metre and the standard gram (the mass of a cubic centimetre of water at 4° centigrade) were officially presented by the scientists to the government. Standard metre bars were made of platinum and distributed throughout the country. However, the new system was not made compulsory, which led to a very muddled state of affairs until, in 1837, the French Parliament decided that the metric system must be the only system used in France.

Within forty years an international organization was set up to unify and improve the metric system, which had begun to be used in other parts of the world. In October 1960 the Eleventh General Conference on Weights and Measures decided that the metre should be defined as the length equal to 1,650,763.73 wavelengths in vacuum of the radiation corresponding to the transition between the levels $2p_{10}$ and $5d_5$ of the Krypton-86 atom. And so the business of getting more and more accurate measurement goes on.

Back in 1790 the French asked the British to join in with their new system of weights and measures. It has taken the British nearly two hundred years to agree to change.

Mural of land measurement in ancient Egypt

LOCKS AND KEYS

*"Mr Yale picked
my ten-tumbler lock,
the finest of its kind,
for which I paid
three hundred dollars"*

Primitive Egyptian lock
and door

A notorious London burglar serving a sentence on board one of His Majesty's prison ships at Portsmouth heard about Jeremiah Chubb's wonderful new lock—the "convict-defying detector lock"—which no one could pick. "Give me the lock and I'll pick it as easily as I've picked any other lock," he challenged. The prison authorities gave him Mr Chubb's lock, all the tools he needed, and even a duplicate of the lock to see how it worked. The government promised him a free pardon if he succeeded, and Chubb promised him £100 reward. The convict worked day after day on the lock. After two and a half months he gave up in despair, and was probably packed off to the Australian colonies.

A serious robbery at the Portsmouth Naval Dockyard in 1817 had so frightened everyone that the government offered a reward of £100 to the inventor of a lock which could not be opened except by its own key. Jeremiah Chubb's lock won.

Locks and keys are like the arms race. Pick a lock and a better one needs to be invented. People have wanted to keep other people away from their possessions for thousands of years. Locks and keys are such an old invention that no one knows when, or where, they began. Strangely enough, the same kinds of locks were used all over the world, from Zanzibar to Indonesia, from Greece to China to the Faeroe Islands above Scotland. The lock design used by the ancient Egyptians five thousand years ago is still found today in rural areas of Egypt, and around the Mediterranean.

It is easy to see how locks developed from a bar of wood or bolt across a door. The trouble with a bolt is that you can shut it from the inside, but how do you open it from the outside? At first, people cut a hand-sized hole through the door. Later, a much smaller hole was made, so that a long wood or metal prodder—a "key"—could be used to push the bolt. An important invention was a row of pegs, small movable pieces of wood or metal called tumblers, which fell by their own weight into the bolt, holding it securely. The key was fitted with a row of corresponding prongs which pushed the tumblers up, releasing the bolt. Later, springs were invented, to hold the tumblers in place. Each key could now be specially designed to fit its own lock. The stem of the key was like an arm and the prongs were like fingers. A key for this kind of lock was often so heavy it had to be carried over the shoulder.

Expert locksmiths in medieval times made beautiful,

elaborate locks and keys for church doors and document chests and city gates. King Henry VIII of England had a large lock, over a foot long, which was screwed to his bed-chamber door wherever he went. Locksmiths always made the key first, then designed a lock to fit it. Each was made by hand, crafted from metal, which meant that no two sets of lock and key were ever quite the same.

Locks and keys altered very little in design, or in the way they were made, until about two hundred years ago, when several English inventors thought out important improvements. The greater the number of complicated pieces inside a lock which have to be moved to certain precise positions by the key, before it can be opened, the safer it is. Jeremiah Chubb's "convict-defying detector lock" had a special lever which was activated, and jammed the mechanism, every time the wrong key was used. Later versions of his lock had six such levers.

A generation before Chubb, a Yorkshire farmer's son called Joseph Bramah came to London to work as a cabinet-maker. But Bramah's head was full of ideas for machines. Londoners were panicking about sensational burglaries—nothing in the city was safe. In 1784 Bramah designed a revolutionary security lock. But a smear campaign was started: Bramah's lock was reputed to be no good. An advertisement, for example, in the morning papers advised people not to break down doors if they lost the key to their Bramah lock. Just contact the advertiser, who would gladly come and pick it. So Bramah improved the design of

An indicating lock of cast and engraved brass, signed Johannes Wilkes de Birmingham Fecit. c.1680

his lock, then issued a public challenge. He put a handsome four-inch iron padlock in the window of his London shop with this message engraved on its face:

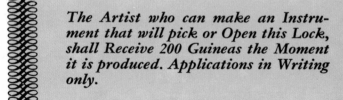

The Artist who can make an Instrument that will pick or Open this Lock, shall Receive 200 Guineas the Moment it is produced. Applications in Writing only.

Only one challenger tried, and he gave up after a week. Bramah's lock became world-famous.

Joseph Bramah now found that his workmen, using traditional tools and methods, could not turn out locks like the original quickly enough to meet the big demand. Such a complicated precision instrument as his lock needed specially designed tools to make it. Bramah, who became a leading inventor of industrial machines, was the first to manufacture locks using machine tools.

The final changeover from locks and keys being hand-crafted and individually made to being mass-produced and machine-made came with the inventions of an American, Linus Yale, Jr, in the 1850s. Yale wanted to be a portrait painter but began, like his father, to design splendid burglar-proof bank locks with names such as Yale's Magic Infallible Bank Lock and Yale's Double Treasury Bank Lock. In 1861 he took out the first patent on his most famous lock, and probably the most popular ever made—the revolutionary Yale cylinder lock. The principle of this lock has never needed to be changed.

Yale wanted to invent an improved security door lock, with a handy, small-sized key, that would be cheap and easily available. To manufacture his locks and keys, Yale used the system, already highly developed in the United States, of interchangeable parts. One man no longer made a complete object, as craftsmen had done for thousands of years. Instead, an object was divided up into all its component parts, and one man concentrated on making just one part. Each time he made that one part it was identical with the last time, because he used specially designed precision machines. Workmen no longer had to be skilled, or even have any idea of the final product, for this could now be assembled out of any selection of each of the component parts. Thousands of identical clocks and guns were already being produced in American factories by these mass-production methods. Soon, the mass-production of sewing-machines and typewriters would be made possible by the same method of interchangeable parts. Linus Yale took the system a stage further by being the first to use mass-production methods to make *unidentical* articles, because each set of lock and key had to differ from the last. The five notches in a Yale key, cut automatically to eight different depths in a milling machine, give 32,768 variations.

Sixty years after Joseph Bramah put his Challenge Lock in the window of his London shop, a young American called Alfred Hobbs came to London's great Crystal Palace Exhibition. Hobbs wanted to publicize the champion Parautoptic Lock made by his company back home in New York. It was displayed at the exhibition. He decided to squash his British competitors by picking their locks. In front of a horrified audience, the latest model Chubb Lock was picked in twenty-five minutes. Hobbs now took up the Bramah Company's challenge. Week after hot summer week he worked, in secret, a few hours a day, until at last he had it open. Bramah's claimed he broke the rules, but paid him the two hundred guineas, and immediately put a new challenge lock in their window, this time made out of steel instead of iron. Down at the Crystal Palace Exhibition, Hobbs laid two hundred shiny new golden guineas on a velvet cloth next to his company's locks, and the crowds thronged to see them.

But the Parautoptic Lock suffered its own terrible defeat five years later when Linus Yale picked model after model with only a wooden key. "Mr Yale," wrote a New York banker, "picked my ten-tumbler lock, the finest of its kind, for which I paid three hundred dollars . . . he cut a wooden key solely from inspection of the lock through the key-hole, which turned the lock back as readily as my key would have done. And then to complete my discomfiture, he cut away one bit of his wooden key and locked it so that I could never have unlocked it with my own key."

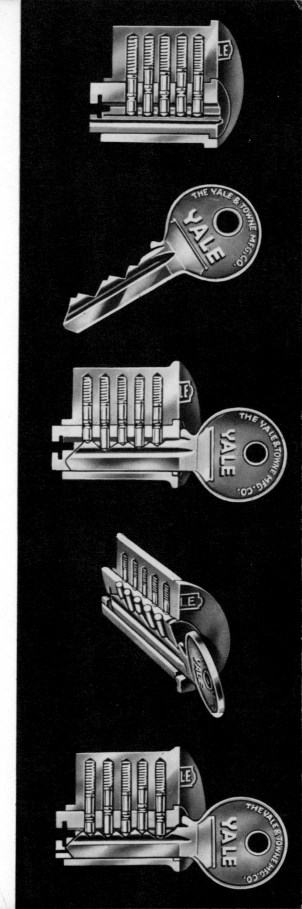

FORKS

"...seeing all men's fingers are not alike cleane"

No one quite knows when we started to use forks, but they are a fairly recent invention. Knives, on the other hand, are as old as man's need to cut and kill. They were made of whatever was found hard and sharp enough: bone and chipped stone and, later, bronze and iron. The first spoons were probably curved shells.

Thomas Coryate used a fork in England in 1609, to spear food and put it in his mouth. On his travels he had seen Italians eat this way and thought it a good idea, though back home he was laughed at. Italians had been using forks for some time. "The reason of this," wrote Coryate, "is the Italian cannot by any means endure to have his dish touched with fingers, seeing all men's fingers are not alike cleane."

A book on table manners written five hundred years ago told people not to grab their food with both hands, but pick it up politely with three fingers only. Another book warned children not to take food with the hand they used to blow their nose. Food at this time in Europe was chopped up at table with a knife. Usually the knife had a sharp, pointed end so that you could skewer the meat and put it in your mouth. A fork was occasionally used to hold the meat down while chopping off chunks, or for serving.

Most men owned just one knife, which hung at their belt ready for everything. One day it would carve the joint and the next it might carve an enemy's throat. Only the wealthy nobles had special sets of knives for eating.

Even after forks were introduced, many of the nobles in Europe continued to use their fingers. In the seventeenth century a knife and fork, or two knives, made a good wedding present for a bride. They hung at her girdle in a decorated sheath. When the rich went travelling they carried

The earliest silver fork owned by the Victoria and Albert Museum in London, was made in 1632/3.

14

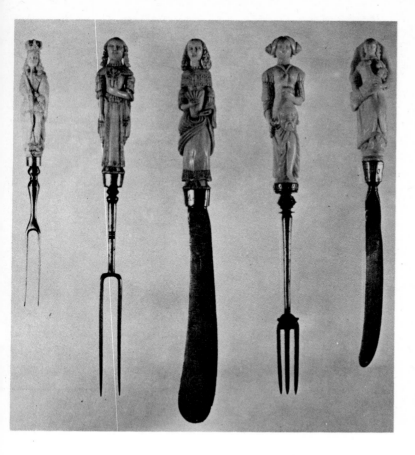

This beautiful set with carved ivory handles was made in 1680. The ladies are wearing dresses of the time of King Charles II.

their own set of knife, fork and spoon with them. Most inns did not provide any.

Forks are mainly a European habit. The Chinese and Japanese, for example, use chopsticks. There is a story about a Chinese visitor who was invited to use a fork by his English host. "This fork," said the Chinese gentleman, "may have been in hundreds of mouths before mine, and among them possibly that of my enemy. The idea is repugnant to me."

The tuning fork is used by musicians to help tune their instruments. It was invented in 1711 by John Shore, a trumpeter in the orchestra of George Frederick Handel.

15

SPECTACLES

"Disks for the eyes"

The inventor of spectacles probably lived in the town of Pisa, Italy, around 1286, and was almost certainly a craftsman working in glass. But nobody knows his name. We only know this much about him because Friar Giordano preached a sermon one Wednesday morning in February 1306 at a church in Florence. "It is not yet twenty years since there was found the art of making eye-glasses which make for good vision," said the Friar, "one of the best arts and most necessary that the world has. So short a time is it since there was invented a new art that never existed. I have seen the man who first invented and created it, and I have talked to him." We know what Friar Giordano said because admirers copied his sermons down as he gave them.

The inventor of spectacles apparently kept the method of making them to himself. Perhaps he thought this was the best way of getting money from his invention. But the idea soon got around. As early as 1300, craftsmen in Venice, the centre of Europe's glass industry, were making the new "disks for the eyes". Spectacles at first were only shaped for far-sighted people. Concave lenses, for short-sighted people, were not developed until the late fifteenth century.

Spectacles allowed people to go on reading and studying long after bad eyesight would normally have forced them to give up. They were like a new pair of eyes. The inventor of such a valuable thing should be honoured, everyone thought. But for centuries no one had any idea who the inventor really was. So all kinds of candidates were put forward: Dutch, English, German, Italians from rival cities. A fake memorial was erected last century in a church in

The earliest known picture of anyone wearing spectacles. Tommaso da Modena painted this picture of Hugh of St Cher in 1352. But Hugh could never have actually worn spectacles because he died nearly one hundred years earlier, before spectacles had been invented. The artist gave Hugh spectacles because they were familiar-enough things in 1352.

Florence to honour a man as the true inventor of spectacles —but he never even existed!

Only recently have researchers dug back through the records, pushed away all the stories and legends, and found the man whose name they do not know and to whom Friar Giordano talked, probably in Pisa, nearly seven hundred years ago. "The world has found lenses on its nose without knowing whom to thank," wrote one researcher.

Spectacles reached China in the fifteenth century. But long before this some Chinese judges had worn a kind of spectacle, made of smoky-coloured quartz. These were worn not to help the judges to see better, but to hide the expression in their eyes in court cases when evidence was being given.

FALSE TEETH

Suddenly he let his false teeth spring out onto the end of his tongue

We cannot replace much of ourselves. But people have always wanted new teeth if their own fell out. Two thousand five hundred years ago Etruscan craftsmen made elegant false teeth out of gold and bone to fit in next to existing ones. Dental decay goes back to before Neolithic times; bad teeth are one of man's oldest miseries.

Although the need to replace decaying or missing teeth has always been great, comfortable and efficient false teeth are very recent. There were three problems: what material to use, how to keep them in the mouth, and how to make them look natural. The Etruscans' skill in designing and making teeth was not matched until the last century. Improvements were very slow, and false teeth were not popular. For a long time they were a luxury. Most people just suffered. Gaps and bad teeth were accepted as a necessary evil, and not much was known about how to keep the mouth clean. Dental work was often done by strong rogues, tooth-drawers, who travelled around the country pulling teeth, especially at fairs. Or it was done by elegant practitioners who looked after the rich and charged a great deal for their services. In England, until a law was passed in 1921, anyone — no matter how ignorant and untrained — could say he practised dentistry.

History books leave teeth out. But the health of kings, generals and politicians is important. It often affects what they decide to do, and that can affect millions of people. Rotten, aching teeth made the sufferers feel very ill and bad-tempered. Queen Elizabeth I often had to make decisions in agony, caused by dreadful toothache. False teeth were very rare in England at this time, but the Queen occasionally wore some when she appeared before her subjects. Poor George Washington suffered first from bad teeth, then, when they were gone, from his false teeth. They were uncomfortable, hurt when he ate, and slurred his speech when he talked. A difficult problem for a President of the United States. Portraits painted of Washington show his mouth in very unnatural positions, caused by his badly fitting teeth. People said he was "anxious and melancholy". No wonder!

Washington's false teeth were made of ivory. Ivory, especially from the walrus or hippopotamus, was the most popular material for making teeth and the bases to carry them. Usually a row of teeth were carved out of the same piece. But ivory was not very practical because it began to

George Washington

rot after a short time in the mouth. Gold was popular, but expensive. When expense did not matter, artificial teeth were sometimes made of silver, mother-of-pearl, or even of agate. About two hundred years ago a Frenchman, after much experimenting, invented teeth made from shiny rot-proof porcelain. At first they were dazzling white, so he added various colours to make them look more natural. Individual porcelain teeth are still used a great deal today.

It was always easier just to replace a few teeth rather than the whole lot. Some practitioners were skilled at this kind of repair work, hooking or tying the new teeth to existing ones, or joining them together along the top. For a while it was fashionable to try transplanting other people's teeth into gaps.

The poor often sold their teeth, but the transplant operation was never really successful. Sometimes transplanted teeth lasted five years, but more often they caused infected mouths, then fell out. For a long time there was a big trade in teeth from the dead, which could be fastened to plates and made to fit gaps in the mouth of some sufferer. The victims of war provided a rich source of supply.

The really difficult job was making a complete set of false teeth. How to get them to stay in? Springs were used between the top and bottom plates, which could sometimes end up making the whole lot jump out of the mouth, to everyone's embarrassment. Two missionaries went into the highlands of Fiji, in the middle of last century. They were taken into the fortified village of a very warlike group of Fijians, then put into a hut down a narrow passage. Escape was impossible. They knew this was probably the end for them. As the Chief and his strong men came into the hut, one of the missionaries had an idea. Suddenly he let his false teeth spring out onto the end of his tongue. He flicked them back into his mouth, then they sprang out again. The Fijians were terrified. How was it possible to do this with your teeth? The missionaries must be very powerful magicians. They were permitted to leave immediately.

About the beginning of the nineteenth century an American dentist realized that the principle of atmospheric pressure could be applied to dentistry. If a plate fitted well, with no air between it and the roof of the mouth, atmospheric pressure or suction would keep it in place, helped by adhesion (the sticking-together of two moist surfaces). But it was many more years before dentures were well enough

WANTED FRONT TEETH *for which Two Guineas a piece will be given, by J. Browne, Surgeon and Dentist, No. 6, Nathan-Street, New York. Sept. 29, 1784*

Drawing of toothless old people by Leonardo da Vinci

made for this method to work successfully, and for the awkward springs to be abandoned.

Faces without teeth have a different shape. The nose and chin end up much closer together, as Leonardo da Vinci showed in his drawings of people he saw around him in Italy at the end of the fifteenth century. But early false teeth, especially full sets, were very difficult to eat with. They usually had to be taken out before a meal, in spite of the fact that the main purpose of teeth is to bite and chew up food. False teeth were often worn, in fact, to hide embarrassment, help in pronunciation, make faces keep their normal shape. Vanity, rather than a desire to chew better, made people wear false teeth.

In 1844 a young American dentist called Horace Wells thought of using laughing gas (nitrous oxide) as an anaesthetic. For the first time painless extraction of teeth was possible. Charles Goodyear had just invented vulcanized rubber. Here was a new, easy-to-work material for making the bases to which false teeth could be attached. The rubber could be moulded to fit the shape of the mouth. Now the pain of extracting teeth was gone, and dentures could be made cheaply. False teeth were available to everyone. The demand was enormous, especially in America. Later, another cheap and newly invented base, celluloid, was tried, for rubber had turned out to be far from ideal.

Today, dentures are made of a plastic which can be moulded and coloured realistically to fit each patient's mouth. Now everyone can wear false teeth that look natural and feel comfortable. The best material so far for making false teeth has turned out to be an artificial one.

LIGHTNING CONDUCTORS

The lightning conductor would "be of use to mankind, in preserving houses, churches, ships, &c., from the stroke of lightning"—so wrote its American inventor, Benjamin Franklin. "Fix on the highest part of those edifices, upright rods of iron made sharp as a needle, and gilt to prevent rusting, and from the foot of those rods a wire down the outside of the building into the ground." The lightning conductor was a most useful invention. Village blacksmiths could hammer one out easily, and the design has not changed much to this day. But some people were worried about using them. Should lightning conductors be attached to church steeples? If God meant to strike a church with lightning, then it had better not be stopped. One angry preacher said that all the lightning conducted out of the thunderclouds into the ground by the new conductors would cause earthquakes: the charge had to come out somewhere.

Americans were certainly much quicker to install the new lightning conductor than the English. As Franklin said, "Thunderstorms are much more frequent here than in Europe." There was less damage by lightning in England, and people were not as frightened of it. An argument began in England about whether lightning conductors should have blunt or sharp ends. Franklin advised sharp ends, based on his own experiments, and at last the British government, acting on the advice of a scientific committee, put pointed iron rods on the buildings where army gunpowder was stored—a very important protection. But in 1776 war broke out between Britain and her American colonies. Franklin supported his fellow Americans, who wanted independence. Sharp ends on lightning conductors meant Benjamin Franklin! And that now meant rebellion! King George III of England ordered another committee to study blunt ends versus sharp ends. Again they advised sharp ends. Patriotic George ordered lightning conductors with knobs on their ends to be installed on his Royal Palace. "Change your mind and advise blunt ends," he ordered the head of the committee. "Sire," said the scientist, in a famous reply, "I cannot reverse the laws and operations of nature."

Franklin thought of the lightning conductor while doing experiments, in about 1750, to find out what electricity was. He discovered that electricity was one single fluid and not several, as European thinkers had decided; that lightning was a form of electricity; and that a charge of static elec-

"I cannot reverse the laws and operations of nature"

Benjamin Franklin

tricity tended to leak off a charged object at sharp points.

Some Europeans could not believe that anyone in the far-off, unsophisticated American colonies could make such important discoveries. Benjamin Franklin based all his discoveries on experiments which he carried out with simple kitchen equipment, and objects such as a kite made of wood and a large silk handkerchief. The study of electricity was still only in its beginnings, and Franklin probably saw the problem more clearly because he did not know much of what other people had already done.

Benjamin Franklin was a very practical man. Besides being an inventor, he was a successful publisher, postmaster, diplomat and politician. When he was over seventy years old, he found it very annoying to have one pair of glasses for reading and another for walking, so he invented the first bifocals, spectacles with one lens in the top half for long-distance sight and a stronger lens in the bottom half for close reading. He also invented a grasping device on a long stick to take down books from high shelves in his library; some grocers still use them to reach packets down from high shelves.

FRANKLIN'S EXPERIMENT, JUNE 1752.
Demonstrating the identity of Lightning and Electricity, from which he invented the Lightning Rod.

In Oxford Street, London, there is a shop which hasn't changed for over a hundred years. *James Smith & Sons*, it says over the door in gold lettering, *Ladies Umbrellas, Tropical Sunshades, Garden & Golf Umbrellas, Life Preservers, Dagger Canes, Swordsticks*. It is the oldest and biggest umbrella shop in Europe. One of Queen Victoria's Prime Ministers, Mr Gladstone, used to buy his umbrellas from Smith & Sons. No respectable gentleman at that time would ever go out without his big, black, correctly rolled umbrella. African chiefs visiting London would make a special trip to Smith & Sons to order huge, decorated ceremonial umbrellas for use back home.

But umbrellas are much, much older than you might expect. Ancient Egyptian carvings show Pharaohs sitting on thrones beneath ceremonial umbrellas. According to Chinese legend, the umbrella was invented three thousand years ago by a Chinese lady, but only those of royal blood or high authority were permitted to use one. The King of Burma had many titles; one was "Lord of the Great Parasol", and he alone could use a white umbrella, while officials carried umbrellas of different colours according to how important they were. The Mikado of Japan never appeared in public without his umbrella bearer. When Queen Victoria's son, the Prince of Wales, toured India in 1877, he rode on an elephant beneath a fabulous golden umbrella; as a mark of respect to their ruler's son, Indian princes presented him with umbrellas made of blue silk looped with pearls, and embroidered brocade set with rubies.

The Greeks probably introduced the umbrella into Europe two thousand years ago. Greek ladies liked going for a walk with a slave holding an umbrella over them to keep off the sun. Roman ladies were particularly fond of purple umbrellas, and they were probably the first people to use umbrellas as protection from the rain.

The umbrella kept on being rediscovered, even though the way it works has not changed much from the beginning. During the sixteenth century the Pope decided that an umbrella was a good symbol of dignity and honour, and had one carried over him whenever he appeared in public.

Travellers began to notice the strange new object. Thomas Coryate, who brought the fork back to England with him from Italy, described the Italian umbrellas. "They are made of leather, something answerable to the form of a little canopy, and hooked on the inside with divers little

"...the umbrella is the sign of having no carriage"

Ancient Assyrian umbrella

23

Cartoon published
January 1782

Centre:
Persia late 15th century

Right:
Japanese couple in the
snow

wooden hoopes that extend the umbrella in a pretty large compass. They are used especially by horsemen who carry them in their hands when they ride, fastening the end of the handle upon their thighs, and they impart so large a shadow upon them that it keepeth the heat of the sunne from the upper part of their bodies." Umbrella comes from the Latin word *umbra* — shade, via the Italian word *ombrella* —little shade.

Slowly the idea caught on in France, then in England. People brought umbrellas home with them from their travels in China, Italy and Spain. But, at first, carrying an umbrella was not considered the done thing. "Those who wish not to be confounded with the vulgar, prefer the risk of getting wet . . . for the umbrella is the sign of having no carriage." When John MacDonald took his umbrella out with him on the streets of London in 1772, cab drivers shouted after him: "Frenchman, Frenchman, why don't you call a coach?" The cab drivers were worried that umbrellas would take away their business.

That same year a shopkeeper in America bought an umbrella from a ship just back from India. He proudly took it out on the street, but, so the story goes, women were frightened, horses bolted, and children threw stones. It was probably the first umbrella in America. But by the nineteenth century fashionable Americans waited eagerly for shipments of the latest umbrellas and parasols from London and Paris. Elegant ladies now carried parasols of lace and beads, with silken fringes, to protect their faces from the sun. It was certainly not fashionable for ladies to have a suntan.

About 1820 the design of umbrellas began to improve.

Heavy, clumsy frames made of oak or cane were replaced by whalebone and, in 1851, by steel ribs. Coverings changed from sticky oiled silk or linen to cotton, alpaca and, much later, nylon.

When English manufacturers first began making umbrellas at the end of the eighteenth century, they often hung little acorns on the handles. It was an old superstition. Acorns were meant to protect against lightning, because the oak-tree was sacred to the God of Thunder. Over in America, Benjamin Franklin had done some important research on lightning, and had invented the lightning conductor. The Frenchman who translated Franklin's book into French was so frightened of lightning that he attached a miniature lightning conductor to the top of his umbrella. He appeared in the streets of Paris in 1786, a wire dangling from his umbrella to the earth, trailing along behind him as he walked.

India, the Maharajah of Mysore, in 1846

Right:
A state umbrella in Nigeria in 1956

Cambodian farmer

25

RUBBER

Hancock kept the masticator a secret, and made his workmen call it the "pickle"

"The king took much Delight in seeing the sport at Ball . . . The Ball was made of the Gum of a Tree that grows in hot Countries, which having Holes made in it distils great white Drops, that soon harden, and being work'd and moulded together turn as black as Pitch. The Balls made thereof tho' hard and heavy to the Hand did bound and fly as well as our Footballs, there being no need to blow them. . . ."

ANTONIO DE HERRERA TORDESILLAS,
Sixteenth Century Spanish Chronicler.

Charles Goodyear agreed that it really wasn't possible to *eat* rubber; or sleep in it. But rubber could be used for everything else, he argued. Charles Goodyear was a man obsessed with an idea. For years he experimented with

rubber, talked about it, thought about it. The joke went around: "If you meet a man who has on an India rubber cap, stock, coat, vest and shoes, with an India rubber money purse, without a cent of money in it, that's Charles Goodyear!" Goodyear believed that he alone was meant to solve the problem of rubber and make it useful.

A lot of people were excited about rubber. Here was a natural product, got by collecting the milky juice which oozed out of cuts in certain trees growing wild in the tropical forests of Central and South America. It was waterproof. It was elastic. It was springy, airtight, and could be moulded into any shape. There was nothing like it. But—and here was rubber's problem—in cold weather it went as hard as a board, and heat made it soft and sticky. Anything made from rubber could become useless overnight.

A chieftain standing before the ball court on two burning rubber balls, from an ancient Mexican picture-writing

Claude Richard, eminent French botanist, saw rubber-trees in flower, 1785, and described the tree for the first time in correct botanical terms in a paper from which this illustration comes.

27

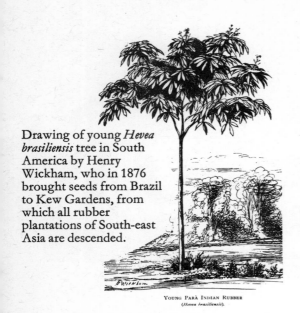

Drawing of young *Hevea brasiliensis* tree in South America by Henry Wickham, who in 1876 brought seeds from Brazil to Kew Gardens, from which all rubber plantations of South-east Asia are descended.

YOUNG PARÀ INDIAN RUBBER
(*Hevea brasiliensis*).

The milky juice from the rubber-tree is called latex. But latex quickly coagulates, so objects had to be made out of rubber on the spot. For centuries Indians in Central and South America had formed it into various shapes for their own use: waterproof cloaks, shoes, balls for their games, and bottles. The best rubber was made by dipping a stick over and over again in latex, and drying each layer in the smoke from a fire. Rubber usually reached Europe or the United States in the shape of a ball or bottle. So one of the first things that Europeans did was try to find something that rubber would dissolve in, to get it back to its original liquid form. Then it could be reshaped.

About the beginning of the last century a new way of lighting houses and streets was found: by coal gas. One of the by-products of burning coal for gas was naphtha, and a Scotsman called Charles Macintosh discovered in 1819 that naphtha was an excellent solvent for rubber. He painted the resulting rubber solution on material to make a waterproof cloth. To get over the problem of stickiness, Macintosh joined two layers of the cloth together, rubber sides inwards like a sandwich. The material was very stiff and heavy, but it did make the first raincoats or "macintoshes".

Meanwhile, in London, Thomas Hancock sliced up rubber bottles, which he got from South America, to make rubber bands. He also stitched thin strips of rubber on material to use as elastic sections in gloves, boots, braces, waistcoat backs, and tops for pockets "to prevent their being picked". Only part of each lump of rubber could be cut up in this way, so in 1820 Hancock invented a machine to help him use all the spare bits. He knew that shreds of rubber, if heated, could be stuck end-to-end to form one long piece. His "masticator" was meant to tear up all the waste rubber, but instead, to Hancock's surprise, the heat from the machine moulded the rubber pieces back into a solid mass. Hancock kept the masticator a secret, and made his workmen call it the "pickle" to throw anyone else off the scent of his invention.

Things made on the spot out of latex lasted fairly well. But once rubber had been softened by heat, or grinding, or a solvent, it lost a great deal of its strength and quickly deteriorated. How could rubber be treated to stay strong, elastic, smooth, unsticky, flexible—to retain all its good properties?

American manufacturers became very enthusiastic about the possibilities of rubber in the early 1830s. Tens of thousands of pairs of overshoes were being imported into the country, made by Amazon Indians directly onto wooden lasts supplied by the Americans. But the market was also being flooded with goods made in American factories: waterproof coats, rubber life-preservers, wagon covers, hose-piping. These goods were made up from treated rubber: the usual coagulated rubber dissolved in turpentine, a most unsatisfactory solvent. Manufacturers scrambled to get in on the big rubber boom without bothering to find out whether the claims for their products were correct. Inevitably the waterproof coats became sticky and smelt horribly, the boots stiffened and cracked, suspenders sagged embarrassingly, hose-pipes perished. The public became sick of rubber, and before long no business man would invest money in it.

Charles Goodyear was walking past a shop in New York City when he saw a rubber life-preserver in the window. He had always been fascinated by the problem of saving life at sea, so he went inside to have a better look. It seemed pretty obvious that the life-preserver would be greatly improved by a better valve. Goodyear was thirty-three years

Hancock's first masticating machine, around 1820

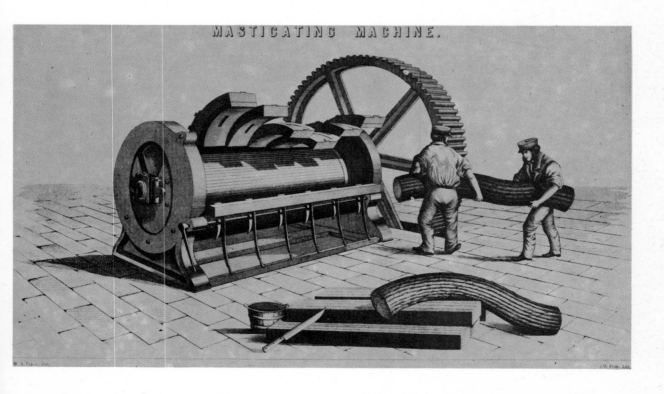

MASTICATING MACHINE.

old, and out of a job. His father's most successful hardware business, the invention and sale of farm implements, had suddenly collapsed, leaving all the Goodyears poor. Charles designed a better valve for the life-preserver; he thought the manufacturers would probably pay him well, but when he took it back to the New York shop, the salesman sadly shook his head. "It's no good inventing a better valve, because the rubber isn't good enough for the one it has already!" he said, and confided to Goodyear all the difficulties, all the frustrations of this maddening, marvellous material called rubber. His company would pay almost anything for the secret of how to solve rubber's problems. There and then Charles Goodyear became dedicated to rubber.

That was in 1834. For the next five years Goodyear experimented. He had no training as a chemist, no equipment and usually no money. His family became poorer, one by one their household goods were pawned, and Goodyear was often in jail for debt. His friends nagged at him to give it all up and get a respectable job as a hardware merchant, which was what he was trained to do. Goodyear was always

Illustrations of articles made from or incorporating natural rubber, from Hancock's book *The Origin and Progress of the Caoutchouc*, published 1857

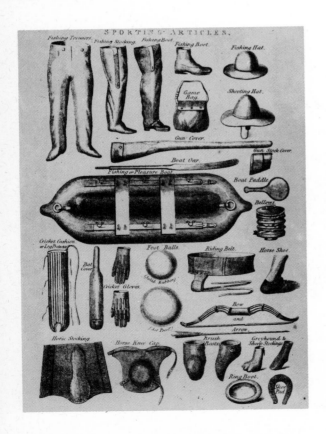

a rather pale and sickly man. But he became much more ill and tired as month after month he shredded specimens of rubber with his fingers, kneaded them in the solvent, added first one substance, then another, to see what would happen, then nailed the rubber mixtures around the house to watch the effect of heat or cold on them. His patient wife suffered it all. Goodyear wore clothes made of his latest examples of "gum-elastic" to test their strength in everyday conditions. Now and then success would seem to come. "I've done it," Goodyear would tell everyone—journalists, friends, investors, and anyone who would listen. He would get a lease on one of the old rubber factories and start turning out a wide range of goods in his wonderful rubber. Things would get better for the Goodyear family. Goodyear made big plans. Then back would come the goods from angry customers, perished and useless as usual. The change Goodyear was hoping to bring about in rubber proved each time to be only temporary.

The worst fiasco was the big mailbags scoop. Goodyear got an important contract to make a hundred and fifty mailbags for the United States government, using his latest "acid gas" technique. "Mr Goodyear appears to have completely succeeded in preparing a fabric of entire flexibility . . . impervious to air or water, and neither stiffened by cold nor fused by heat," reported a Boston newspaper. Goodyear left the finished mailbags hanging in the factory by their handles and went away on business. When he got back there they were, sagging, stretched and sticky. The new process was only surface-deep; it could not penetrate right through the rubber. After this, no one took any more notice of Charles Goodyear and his prophecies about rubber. If he had died without succeeding, Charles Goodyear would have been forgotten as a crank.

Some time later, Goodyear revisited the factory with some companions and decided to try the effect of heat on a piece of the mailbag rubber mixture on which he had pinned so much faith Carelessly he dropped it on a hot stove. Instead of melting, as usual, the rubber unexpectedly charred, like leather. Excitedly Goodyear held another piece of the rubber mixture in front of a fire. It charred again, but Goodyear could see a thin edge of rubber between the burn and the original material, which looked and felt exactly right. Goodyear had now done enough work and experimenting to know what he was looking for. He was convinced that

Charles Goodyear

here was the answer. But none of the others with him was impressed. It was just another of Goodyear's claims for his experiments.

In fact, Goodyear had made the first piece of vulcanized rubber. He called his discovery "metallic gum-elastic", but the change he had achieved in raw rubber came to be called "vulcanization" after Vulcan, mythical god of fire.

The piece of rubber that fell on the stove was made up of a mixture of rubber, sulphur and white lead. Sulphur turned out to be the essential ingredient, though the white lead helped to speed up the process of change or "curing". Heating was equally essential, but the question now was, how much heat and for how long? Goodyear became more obsessed than ever. He had solved the rubber problem, but no one would take any notice of his discovery. He was determined that people must be made to realize its importance. Otherwise the knowledge might die with him, and rubber's marvellous possibilities would go on being unused. Now he had to find out exactly how to achieve the process of vulcanization satisfactorily, every time.

Goodyear made his discovery of vulcanization in January 1839. The next five years were even worse than the first five. Goodyear worked more and more feverishly, and the family was so poor he even had to sell his children's schoolbooks to buy food. He experimented endlessly with ways of heating the rubber mixture. As soon as his wife had finished baking the bread, Goodyear was in the kitchen using the heated oven. He boiled the rubber in saucepans, roasted it directly in the hot ashes of the fire, cooked it by steam from the kettle's spout. He tried heating for one hour, six, twenty-four. Occasionally he would get a small, well-cured sample, but then he failed to repeat it.

Goodyear begged heating space for his experiments from anyone in the village—the blacksmith, the local factory owner. "He used to give me considerable unnecessary trouble . . . by attending to his samples, and by keeping the furnace door of my fire open from time to time frequently," complained one of the factory workmen. "He used to be fussing about with those samples," said another, "and I thought it was silly and boys' play like, and I used to laugh at it. I used to be sorry for him." Everyone knew that heating was one thing which ruined rubber and made it sticky. And here was Goodyear trying to convince them that heating was essential. With a little borrowed money,

Charles Goodyear's Exhibition of Hard India Rubber Goods at the Crystal Palace, England, 1851.

Goodyear managed to build a large brick oven. The rubber charred under the intense heat. So he tried rolling strips of rubber through the top of the furnace. It came out in sections, some blistered, some sticky and uncured, and some just right.

Goodyear received a patent for his process in June 1844. He couldn't afford to get one earlier. But by that time Thomas Hancock in England had seen a sample of Goodyear's rubber, managed to work out with hundreds of hurried experiments what had been done to it, and had taken out English patents for the process. In America, once the value of vulcanization was established, Goodyear found himself up against a horde of imitators, patent infringers and people who claimed he had not invented vulcanization at all.

Once again people raced and fought to make fortunes from rubber. There were enormously expensive law cases about the invention. Certainly several other men—in Germany and Holland, for example—had added sulphur to rubber before Goodyear. But none had any real understanding of what they had done, or of the part heat had to play.

Sick, tired Goodyear was buffeted by attacks on his truthfulness, and his patents. But probably he did not really care about making a fortune. His only interest continued to be promoting rubber. He spent his time and money developing new uses for his great love, then selling the methods to manufacturers who proceeded to make millions of dollars from his ideas. Goodyear lavished $30,000 on an elaborate three-room pavilion, Goodyear's Vulcanite Court, at London's Crystal Palace Exhibition. Everything was made of rubber: walls, furniture, carpets, curtains, pictures, musical instruments, even rubber combs and buttons. Visitors marvelled, and Goodyear won a Grand Council Medal for his "unique and ingenious" designs, but none of it earned him any money. When Goodyear died in 1860 his finances were in a dreadful muddle, and he was probably in debt. Yet the public resented him. He must be a millionaire, they thought. Everything made of rubber seemed to have the name Goodyear on it.

In 1889 the audience at a Belfast cycle track roared and laughed when they saw one of the competitors entering the arena on a bicycle with two smallish identical-size wheels. Over the squat bicycle towered the other competitors, balanced proudly on their racing penny-farthings — bicycles with a huge wheel in front and a tiny wheel behind. But the seemingly ludicrous bicycle won easily. It was fitted with pneumatic tyres. A hollow rubber tube inflated with air under pressure turned out to give a faster and smoother ride than a solid rubber tyre. Dr John Dunlop, a Belfast veterinary surgeon, had the year before designed a prototype pneumatic tyre from garden hose-pipe for his ten-year-old son's bicycle. In fact, the pneumatic tyre had been invented forty-three years earlier by a young Scotsman, Robert William Thomson. "Thomson's aerial wheels" were tested very satisfactorily in London's Hyde Park, but no one was interested and they were forgotten.

Since Goodyear's discovery of vulcanization, rubber had been used for making a range of things: waterproof footwear, clothing, and surgical and engineering appliances. But the development of the bicycle and later the motor-car with their pneumatic tyres, helped to turn rubber into a giant industry. Even sixty years after Goodyear's discovery,

very little research had been carried out on the chemistry of rubber. Each manufacturer worked by rule of thumb, combining ingredients and curing the rubber by his own secret formula without really knowing why it worked. But motor-car tyres needed to be made of consistent, high-performance rubber. Research into rubber processing now became more and more important to manufacturers, and out of this research plus the needs of expanding industry came an increasing range of new uses for rubber. Rubber was now a vital raw material.

Rubber collected in Central and South America from wild trees differed tremendously in quality. In 1876 an Englishman managed to gather seeds from the best rubber-trees he could find, in the highlands of Brazil, and ship them by fast steamer to England. The seeds were grown in special containers at the Kew Botanical Gardens in London, and those that germinated were shipped to Ceylon the next year. From these seeds, and others gathered in the same way, came the enormous rubber plantations of Malaya, Ceylon, Indonesia, the West Indies.

Rubber was so vital a raw material that capturing areas of rubber plantation became an important wartime objective. And even before the Second World War, scientists were working hard on developing synthetic rubbers. Goodyear never expected his experiments to end up improving the original latex, but they did. Today, chemists can build in certain properties to each type of synthetic rubber and produce a type of made-to-measure rubber for each particular job. Yet natural, vulcanized rubber is still the best material available for many jobs.

John Dunlop, with one of the earliest pneumatic-tyred bicycles

CHEWING-GUM

The wild sapodilla-tree

Leaves and fruit of the sapodilla-tree

The Maya Deity, Kukulcan, the gum-chewing god

Mix together some corn syrup, plenty of sugar, a little flavour like peppermint oil, and the juice of the sapodilla-tree. Roll the doughy mixture out into thin sheets, cut them up into sticks or pellets, wrap each one up in bright paper. Every American chews on average three hundred pieces a year, every Briton a hundred, every Japanese two hundred.

Indians in Central America discovered probably at least a thousand years ago that chicle was good to chew. It oozed out of cuts in the wild sapodilla-tree, thick and milky, in much the same way as rubber trickles out of rubber-trees. One hundred years ago an American called Thomas Adams, Jr, tried to use chicle to make rubber. It did not work, so he decided to use his chicle to make chewing-gum. That was not very successful either, until he thought of asking shopkeepers to give away a piece of chewing-gum every time a customer bought some sweets. Soon people were asking for chewing-gum by itself, especially after Adams added sugar and flavouring.

William Wrigley, Jr, became very rich in the same sort of way. He began by working in his father's factory. As a sales gimmick he gave away packets of chewing-gum with every order of baking-powder he received from grocers. When he noticed that the chewing-gum was more popular than the baking-powder, he decided to make and sell chewing-gum himself. Wrigley ended up with factories in the United States, Germany, Australia and Britain making Spearmint, Juicy Fruit, PK, for the whole world to chew.

THE SAFETY RAZOR

"The thing to do is invent something which people have to have, but which they can use, throw away, then buy another one."

In the days when King Camp Gillette was a travelling salesman, he thought hard about this statement — made by the man who invented the disposable bottle cap. "I was a dreamer," he said, "who believed in the 'gold at the foot of the rainbow' promise." He was forty when the great idea came to him one morning, while he was shaving. A razor with a cheap disposable blade! Men shaved with a razor and blade all in one, and the blade had to be re-sharpened whenever it got blunt. That was quite often, for each time the average man shaves, he slices off approximately twenty-five thousand bristles — the equivalent of seven yards. Why not invent a razor blade so cheap that it could be fastened into a special holder and, when no longer sharp, could simply be thrown away and replaced by a new one? "I rushed out," said Gillette, "and bought some pieces of brass, some steel ribbon used for clock springs, a small hand vice and some files." With these he built the first rough model.

That was in 1895. Gillette had the idea, now he had to develop it. For the next six years he struggled with ways of making a cheap, wafer-thin blade. He needed very thin, very strong steel. But he had no technical training; steel experts thought the whole idea was impossible, and friends laughed at him. Then, luckily, he met an ingenious inventor called William Nickerson, who agreed to work on the mechanical problems. Nickerson had already invented such things as the push-button mechanism which stops a lift at a certain floor, and machinery for automatically weighing and packing cereals.

The first Gillette Safety Razor company was started in 1901, above a fish shop by the Boston wharves.

William Nickerson solved all the design problems, and, just as important, invented special machinery to make the razors and blades automatically. But the company was in dreadful difficulties: it owed money, and no one would buy the razors. Gillette and Nickerson gave them away to their friends, and at last one friend recognized what a good idea the invention was and promised financial backing. It was the turning-point. In 1903, 51 razors and 168 blades were produced. Next year (when Gillette got the patent for his design) the total rose to 90,000 razors

"I rushed out and bought some pieces of brass, some steel ribbon used for clock springs, a small hand vice and some files"

"A Sufferer for Decency", from an 18th century print

A NEW SHAVING MILL, WHICH WILL SHAVE SIXTY CUSTOMERS IN ONE MINUTE.

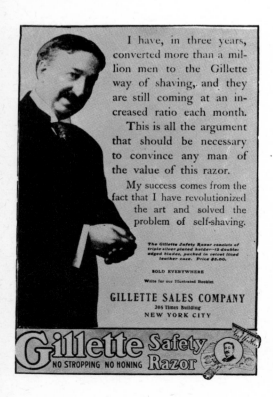

and 124,000 blades. In 1908 just under 300,000 razors and over 13 million blades were sold. In 1909 Gillette had factories in England, France, Germany and Canada and was so successful he retired to California, where he grew fruit-trees and dreamt about reorganizing the world's economy. His face — with dark wavy hair and neat moustache — continued to appear on the front of every packet of Gillette razor blades until 1963.

Men have been shaving their faces for thousands of years. Bronze-age men used bronze razors, which, along with their weapons and jewellery, were often buried with them. The Indians of Central America used a sharp, glassy rock called obsidian. Even pumice stone has been tried, to grind the whiskers down. Throughout history, shaving has been in and out of fashion. Sometimes it was banned for religious reasons. On the other hand, soldiers were often discouraged from growing beards, because a beard gave the enemy far too good a hand-hold in battle! The old cut-throat razor was really rather a dangerous weapon — a sharp, unprotected thin blade — and it had to be used with skill. The first safety razor was invented in 1762 by a Frenchman, Jean-Jacques Perret. He put a guard along one side of the blade. It looked rather like a small rake, and stopped the blade from slipping into the skin. An Englishman, William Henson, invented the modern form of safety razor by setting the blade at right-angles to the handle. But safety razors took a long time to become popular.

When Gillette started marketing his safety razor with disposable blades at the beginning of this century, he got involved in a big advertising war with his rivals who made ordinary razors. Barbers were frightened of losing their trade and fought against Gillette's safe "do it yourself" method.

Soon, however, razors with disposable blades were themselves being challenged by an entirely new technique: dry shaving. No soap, no water, no brushes, creams or lotions, just a small machine with a moving cutter rotating or oscillating against a fixed cutter. Hairs pass through the slots of one and are cut off by the other. The first patent for this new technique was taken out by an Englishman, G.P. Appleyard, just before the First World War. In 1923 Colonel Jacob Schick got a patent for the first electric shaver — the dry-shaving method — using a powerful little motor encased in an insulated handle.

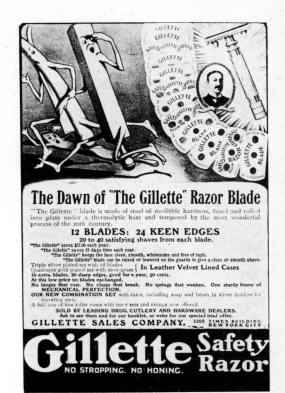

The Dawn of "The Gillette" Razor Blade

"The Gillette" blade is made of steel of neolithic hardness, fused and rolled into plate under a thermolytic heat and tempered by the most wonderful process of the 20th century.

12 BLADES: 24 KEEN EDGES
20 to 40 satisfying shaves from each blade.

"The Gillette" saves $52.00 each year.
"The Gillette" saves 15 days time each year.
"The Gillette" keeps the face clean, smooth, wholesome and free of rash.
"The Gillette" blade can be raised or lowered on the guards to give a close or smooth shave.
Triple silver plated set with 12 blades   } In Leather Velvet Lined Cases
Quadruple gold plated set with monogram }
10 extra blades, 20 sharp edges, good for a year, 50 cents.
At this low price no blades exchanged.
No hinges that rust. No clasps that break. No springs that weaken. One sturdy frame of MECHANICAL PERFECTION.
OUR NEW COMBINATION SET with razor, including soap and brush in silver holders for traveling men.
A full line of fine toilet cases with razor sets and fittings now offered.
SOLD BY LEADING DRUG, CUTLERY AND HARDWARE DEALERS.
Ask to see them and for our booklet, or write for our special trial offer.
GILLETTE SALES COMPANY, 1205 TIMES BUILDING NEW YORK CITY

Gillette Safety Razor
NO STROPPING. NO HONING.

THE SHEARING MACHINE

*Curse the machine
and its inventors!*

Hand shears

The Darling River was in full flood. Muddy brown water sped under the overhanging branches of gum-trees. Sharp eddies swirled above submerged roots caught on the river bottom. Forty angry shearers were camped along one bank. Across the river were the homestead and outbuildings of one of Australia's well-known sheep properties, Dunlop station. There stood the big iron shearing shed, the sheep yards, and 184,000 sheep waiting to be shorn. But the shearers were on strike.

Three weeks earlier, about a hundred men — some of the best shearers in Australia — had gathered for work at Dunlop station. It was June 1888. Shearers were tough workers, humping their swags along bush tracks from station to station during the season, living rough, working hard. The Dunlop manager chose forty of the best men and led them to the shearing shed. There, without any warning, he confronted them with forty newfangled Wolseley shearing machines. The shearers would not touch the machines. They were all experienced with the hand shears and proud of their speed and skill. They crossed the river, set up camp, and waited. And the sheep waited too, in their heavy fleeces, and all the money to be made from the wool stayed on their backs.

Every day of the strike, John Howard and Charlie Sheppard crossed the Darling River and joined in whatever the shearers were doing. They never missed a chance to talk about the advantages of the new shearing machine. John Howard had helped to invent it, and Charlie Sheppard was a champion shearer converted to using and demonstrating it. But the striking shearers knew the years of experience needed to become expert with the hand shears. After all, sheep had been shorn since biblical times with blades: really two knives riveted together. Good blade shearers could shear a hundred and fifty sheep a day — and men were paid on results. John Howard explained that with the machine, just as with shears, sheep still had to be caught and held and the fleece taken off in the proper way. Men still had to be strong yet relaxed, careful and skilful at their job. Anyone could learn to use the new machines in a week, said the shearers. Curse the machine and its inventors! It was a threat.

The discussions were getting nowhere. At the end of the third week several shearers challenged John Howard to swim the flooded Darling River. He did, twice, before breakfast. And that broke the strike. The forty men decided that if Howard was so sporting they would give his machine a try. But things still did not go well. The combs on the shearing machines were broken, someone cut the main pulley belt from the engine, and each shearer turned in a mocking tally of fifty sheep shorn a day. Then two New Zealanders began to get the feel of the shearing machine and raised their total to 100 sheep a day. And one of the champions with the blades, young Jim Davidson, really made his mind up to try. On the fourth day he scored 114 sheep . . . then 173. The race for the highest tally was on — and the shearing machine was a success. The Governor of New South Wales himself came to Dunlop station to watch the shearing shed in action. By the end of the same year, 1888, twenty-two of the biggest stations had installed shearing machines.

The shearing machine was a combined invention. The first ever, "a mechanical contrivance for cutting wool fleece", was patented in 1868 by a Melbourne printer, James Higham. But the man who really made mechanical shearing a commercial success was Frederick Wolseley, brother of the famous British soldier Field-Marshal Lord Wolseley. Frederick came to Australia when he was seventeen and worked on various stations learning the business of sheep-raising. After a few years Wolseley became very interested in the possibilities of shearing machines. The sheep population of Australia was rapidly rising. A few thousand sheep in 1800 became more than one hundred million before the end of the century. In the beginning, sheep were raised for meat. Now their wool was Australia's chief export. Every year river-boats, slow bullock drays, horse-drawn wagons, even camels, brought the huge wool clip in from the country to the railheads and ports. There were not enough skilled shearers to cope with the increasing numbers of sheep. New ways of harvesting the wool needed to be found.

Wolseley's first crude shearing machine took part of the fleece off a sheep in 1872. He gathered skilled men around him to help invent improved models, test them, iron out their defects. In 1883 Wolseley persuaded John Howard, a mechanic newly arrived from England and full of ideas about horse-clippers and shearing machines, to work with him. Two years later they decided it was time to launch the machine. It had been put together in a little

Shearing machines in
action

work-shed on Wolseley's station in New South Wales
with nothing more complicated than a hand-drill, a small
foot lathe, a few tools, and a blacksmith's anvil and forge.

A competition was organized. Wolseley took his two
best shearers, Hassam Ali, a Sudanese, and Jack Joy, to
Melbourne to shear against champion blade shearer Dan
Brown. The judges declared Brown the winner — until
Ali ran the Wolseley shearing machine over the three
hand-shorn sheep and got off another $2\frac{1}{4}$ pounds of wool.
Wool was money; the principle of the shearing machine
was justified. Yet, despite more competitions and public
demonstrations, prejudice against the machine ran high.
For several years Wolseley made little progress selling
either his idea or his machine. When the manager of
Dunlop station decided to equip his shearing shed with
machines in 1888, it was the big breakthrough Wolseley
had worked for. It was here at Dunlop that the first complete
shearing by machine in the world took place.

Jim Davidson, who was converted to using the machine
at Dunlop, joined Wolseley's team as a demonstrator.

Together he and John Howard toured country districts showing disbelieving station owners and shearers how the machine worked. There was much resistance and occasional sabotage. Davidson set a special lightweight demonstration model on a bicycle, and pushed and rode it over miles of sandy country tracks to spread the message of the machine to distant sheep stations. Even the power to run the shears came from the jacked-up bicycle wheel. Davidson tried to time his arrival with the shearing season. The fact that the machine took that extra layer of wool off a sheep was not popular with the shearers.

Frederick Wolseley went back to England to set up his own workshops. Herbert Austin, one of the young mechanics who helped him with the design of the shearing machine in Australia, also went back home to work for Wolseley. Herbert Austin designed and made the first Wolseley car in England in 1895. A few years later he started his own motor works; and so began the famous Austin car, and the career of Lord Austin.

Gradually, more and more shearing sheds went over to machinery. At first, power was supplied by a steam engine. Later oil and petrol engines were used and, finally, electricity.

Shearing machines spread from Australia and New Zealand to the rest of the world. But improvements in machines still tended to come from the practical experience of shearers in Australia and New Zealand. Known as the world's fastest shearers, these professionals fly or drive from one shed to the next during the season. There has always been strong competition between shearers to achieve the highest number of sheep shorn in a working day. The record with blades was set up in Queensland in 1892: 321 merino sheep in seven hours forty minutes. No one beat that, even with a machine, for fifty-five years. Today's champion shearer averages less than a minute and a half to remove the fleece from a merino sheep, on a record day. One of the problems in setting records is that breeds of sheep differ from area to area. This even raises a problem inside Australia, because careful breeding has given the merino a heavier coat. In the 1880s the average greasy weight of the fleece a shearer had to take off was around five to six pounds. In the 1950s it was over nine pounds. But the Australian shearer still reckons he can shear three sheep to the Englishman's one.

Perhaps it will all one day disappear: the hum of machinery, the good smell and action of a working shearing shed, the row of silent men, backs bent over briefly immobile sheep as the mantle of wool falls to the floor under sweeping practised strokes. Recently, researchers in the United States have developed a chemical defleecing agent. A compound called cyclophosphamide given to sheep causes constriction or thinning of the wool fibre just at one point. The whole fleece can be peeled off with no cutting whatever of blade or machine. If this turns out to be practical, then the story of sheep shearing will have come full circle. In very early times, before shears were invented, men pulled the wool off their sheep.

Out on the board the old shearer stands,
Grasping his shears in his thin, bony hands;
Fixed is his gaze on a bare-bellied yoe —
Glory, if he gets her, won't he make the ringer go.

CHORUS:

Click go the shears, boys, click, click, click.
Wide is his blow and his hands move quick.
The ringer looks around and is beaten by a blow,
And curses the old snagger with the bare-bellied yoe.

In the middle of the floor, in his cane-bottomed chair,
Sits the boss of the board with his eyes everywhere,
Notes well each fleece as it comes to the screen,
Saying, "By the living Harry, can't you take 'em off clean?"

The tar-boy is there and awaiting in demand,
With his blackened tar-pot in his tarry hand.
Sees an old sheep with a cut upon its back —
Here is what he's waiting for — it's "Tar here, Jack."

Shearing is all over and we've all got our cheques,
Roll up your swags, boys, we're off on the tracks.
The first pub we come to, it's there we'll have a spree,
And everyone that comes along, it's "Come and drink with me."

A flat iron sheet by itself is not particularly rigid. But bend it into even waves or corrugations and it becomes much stiffer. The people who lived around the Mediterranean two and a half thousand years ago knew about corrugating metal. They made buckets out of hammered corrugated sheets of bronze; some have been dug up recently and put into museums.

An inventor called Joseph Francis found out about corrugating when he tried to make the perfect lifeboat, to save people from a wrecked ship. It was meant to be a kind of enclosed boat and run on a hawser between ship and land. The first model, made of wood, cracked up under the strain. The flat sheets of iron Francis tried next were not strong enough either, so Francis decided they must be corrugated. He spent four or five years working out how to shape corrugated iron to the curves of a boat. After he succeeded, the first corrugated iron lifeboat was installed on a dangerous piece of the American coast facing the Atlantic Ocean. Three years later, in January 1850, a British ship came to grief, and Francis's lifeboat saved 199 out of 200 passengers.

Francis applied his corrugated iron idea to other inventions, especially military vehicles. These included probably the first ever amphibious duck: a watertight army wagon for crossing rivers. He received orders for his inventions from governments all over Europe, and medals for his services to life-saving. The Emperor of Russia ordered a fleet of shallow-draught, corrugated iron steamers, to be transported in pieces over the mountains, and reassembled on the inland Aral Sea. In 1890, when Joseph Francis was eighty-nine years old, the United States Congress awarded him the largest medal they had ever given anyone. It cost six thousand dollars and was made of gold.

About two hundred years ago improved ways of manufacturing sheets of iron meant that it became cheap and plentiful enough to use for all kinds of new purposes. Richard Walker, of Rotherhithe in London's dockland, was probably the first to start corrugating iron sheets, in 1828, although we do not know anything about his methods. In 1833 Walker's Patent Corrugated Iron Factory was listed in the London Post Office Directory, and some of the buildings in the London Docks had corrugated-iron roofs.

Several scientists had worked on ways of stopping iron

Efficient, light, practical, cheap, waterproof

Corrugated iron shanty town

45

from rusting. In 1836 a French chemist called Sorel invented a process for galvanizing iron by dipping it into baths of molten zinc. He did not fully understand why his method protected iron from rusting. In fact, an alloy of zinc and iron was formed, and it was this which resisted corrosion. Eight years later an Englishman, John Spencer, invented the modern method of corrugating a sheet of metal. Instead of using a slow, heavy press that made only one curve at a time, he ran the sheets of iron between specially designed rollers, bending, not stretching, them into shape.

Now people had an efficient, light, practical, cheap, waterproof, new material for outside use. Corrugated galvanized iron was especially suitable for roofs. But there was a great deal of prejudice against it, and corrugated galvanized iron did not look attractive.

Only a few years after it was developed, corrugated iron was being unloaded by the ton on wharves in the Australian colonies. Sheets and sheets of it, shining in the Australian sun, hot to touch. Gold had been discovered in 1851, and thousands of eager gold-diggers poured into Australia from all over the world. Where could they live? Corrugated iron seemed the answer. Settlers used it for the walls and roofs of houses. Two sheets leaning in together at least made a shelter up-country at the goldfields. Large pieces of stringybark stripped off gum-trees had been used to cover many early Australian buildings. Now cheap, easy-to-fix, easily transported corrugated iron was put on top of the old leaking bark roofs.

Cattle-station homestead in Australia

BARBED WIRE

"I wish the man who invented barbed wire had it all wound round him in a ball and the ball rolled into hell." Fence-cutter wars are not often mentioned in cowboy films. But they happened in the real American West less than one hundred years ago. Men drew their guns over barbed wire. Every roll of the ferocious-looking stuff, painted a sticky black or sometimes bright red, meant land fenced in that had never been fenced in before.

HELL BROKE LOOSE IN TEXAS

Wire-cutters Cut 500 Miles in Coleman County

The enemies of barbed wire crept out quietly in the night. A few snips here, a few snips there, and miles of newly strung fencing came down. The rancher who had just paid to put it up fought back. "The fence-cutters themselves have told me," said a Texas Ranger in 1888, "that while a man was putting up his fence one day in a hollow, a crowd of wire-cutters was cutting it behind him in another hollow back over the hill." It was an angry Texan rancher who wished the inventor of barbed wire in hell.

There was war between the inventors of barbed wire, too — they fought in the law courts. Each one said he got the idea first. The Great Barbed Wire Case lasted eighteen years, before the United States Supreme Court decided that old Joseph Glidden of De Kalb, Illinois, was the inventor.

But Jacob Haish, also of De Kalb, built himself a big expensive house and carved over the door, JACOB HAISH. *Inventor of Barb wire.*

It all began one day in 1873. Glidden and Haish, and the owner of the local hardware store, Isaac Ellwood, wandered

along to the De Kalb county fair. Over by the cattle enclosure a salesman was demonstrating a new kind of fencing he had invented. He hung a long strip of wood with spikes sticking out of it along the wire of an ordinary fence. Cattle wouldn't go near the fence — even with dogs yapping and nipping around their heels — because the spikes frightened them.

The local farmers crowded around to watch. Out here in Illinois, fencing interested everyone. Glidden and his neighbours farmed good land on the edge of the great American prairie. The prairie stretched west for a thousand miles, open, gently rolling. Travellers said it looked like a great grassy ocean. But farmers need fences, and none of the usual kind worked on the prairie. Wooden fences were too expensive, because timber had to be brought over from the eastern states. Very few trees grew here in the open. There were not enough rocks to build those patient stone walls men made when they had to. Farmers tried growing hedges, but this was not successful. Some fences were being made out of plain wire, but the wires snapped easily when the temperature changed, and in any case cattle just leant up against them and they broke.

Old Joe Glidden went home from the fair that day and started experimenting with bits of wire. He was thinking about that spiky fence that frightened the cattle. What if he hung barbs and spikes straight onto the wire? He tried various ways, but the barbs would not stay put. One day, as he was picking up the wires, they tangled. Glidden twisted two strands together and bent a short piece of wire between the twists. Here was a man-made thorn hedge! You could see through the wire, it took up little space, made no shade, no weeds would grow along its base, it didn't take goodness from the soil, snow wouldn't drift against it, the twisted wires wouldn't snap when the temperature changed — and it was hard-wearing and cheap. Glidden hurried to patent his invention.

To all whom it may concern: Be it known that I, Joseph F. Glidden, of De Kalb, in the county of De Kalb and state of Illinois, have invented a new and valuable Improvement in Wire-Fences.

In the meantime Jacob Haish and Isaac Ellwood had also invented similar types of fencing. By the time the patents were awarded, it was obvious that barbed wire would make its inventor a fortune, and the long, bitter law cases began.

At first Glidden made his barbed wire at home. He used the farm's grindstone to twist the wires, and he had his wife's coffee mill converted to make the barbs. "We were working in the barn, and would make about forty feet of barb wire at a time," said Andrew Johnson, Mr Glidden's farm-hand. "The next spring, after having made wire in the barn all winter, we made it out of doors in the woods, part of the time on Mr Glidden's farm and afterwards down on the fair grounds." Soon Joe Glidden was renting a factory in De Kalb. One boy climbed the tower of a windmill nearby with a bucket of barbs and another boy carried up a bundle of wires. The barbs were slid down the wires, then the wire taken over to the factory where it was twisted and the barbs spaced.

Back on the east coast of America, a large firm which manufactured plain wire noticed the big orders coming in from De Kalb. They sent an agent to find out what was going on; he came back with samples of the new barbed wire. Without wasting a minute, the firm hired an inventor to design an automatic machine for mass-producing barbed wire. They patented the machine so as to make it difficult for competitors to start up in business. Then the Vice-President of the firm went to De Kalb and bought up Glidden's business. The new automatic machine began working in April 1876 and produced wire at the rate of seventy barbs a minute. Just ten years after Glidden's invention, the barbed-wire factory at De Kalb made six hundred miles of barbed-wire fencing every ten hours. And that was only one factory.

Fast-talking salesmen took the wire out west into Texas, and Wyoming, and New Mexico. At first people were reluctant to try such a newfangled thing. One day John W. "Bet-a-Million" Gates, the greatest barbed-wire salesman of them all, called in at the little town of Mexia, Texas. The owner of the local hardware store, a Mr W. H. Richardson, decided to risk an order of the new wire. But, when it arrived, not even the cowboys dared unload the vicious-looking fencing. "I remember one of the spools got away, or jumped the chute, struck one of the cowboys on the leg and tore half of his boot off." Mr Richardson organized a gala demonstration. People crowded into town from miles around. A row of posts were put up alongside the main road. The barbed-wire spools were loaded onto a farm wagon, the ends of the wire fastened onto the end post and the wagon driven along the row of posts while the wire

Patents for barbed wire

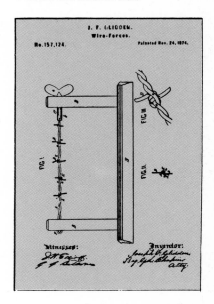

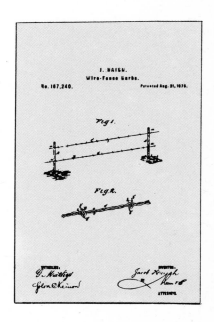

wound off the spools. After going a fair distance, the wagon stopped and one back wheel was jacked up. Helpers fastened the wire around the hub and, by turning the wheel, pulled in the wire till it was taut. All that needed to be done now was to staple the wire to the posts. There stood the storekeeper's new fence put up in double-quick time. A little more persuasion like this, and barbed wire was ordered in train-loads. Ranchmen and farmers just drove to the railway siding and unloaded the spools straight into their wagons.

Joseph Glidden's daughter married a Mr Bush of Chicago. He and another relation of Glidden's, H. B. Sanborn, went west, to the dry uplands and steep-sided canyons of the Texas Panhandle. This was cattle country. Herds of almost wild Texas longhorns roamed the open grassy range — still the hunting-grounds of nomadic Indians. Twice a year, cowboys rounded up the cattle and the ranchmen branded their own. Once a year cattle were driven north along broad stock routes to the railways which took them to Chicago for meat. This was free range country: there were no fences to divide one man's ranch from the next.

Sanborn and Bush wanted to prove the value of barbed wire for big ranches. In 1880 they chose a huge slab of good country in the Texas Panhandle for a ranch. Then, instead of letting the cattle roam free, like other cattlemen, they fenced in the land. The barbed wire had to be brought by wagon freight from the nearest railway terminus, two hundred and fifty miles to the north. Fencing in a hundred and fifty miles of the Frying Pan Ranch cost $39,000. It was the beginning of the end of the free range in the Texas Panhandle.

One day, a man rode his horse along a well-travelled track. The next day, a barbed-wire fence stopped him. Stock were used to roaming free. Many were badly injured before they learnt to avoid the vicious barbs. A brief, violent struggle broke out in Texas, and all over the West, between fencemen and no-fencemen. Between men who wanted the West to stay free, open country, and those who wanted to divide it up behind barbed-wire fences. Where the land was more suited to farming, the fight went on between farmers who now had fences for their fields, and wanted to take land used by the cattlemen, and cattlemen who hated farmers and wanted the prairie to stay cattle country. The fence-cutters often had good reason to do what they did. Big fencemen would sometimes put barbed wire around all the available water, or around land they did not own, or hem in a small farmer and force him out. Barbed wire seemed unnatural and inhuman; the Indians called it the "Devil's Rope". All the same, in a very few years barbed wire changed the American West. "Don't fence me in," sang the cowboy, but fenced in he was, and looking after fences now became one of his jobs.

Only a few years after the fence-cutter wars in the American West, barbed wire was being used for real war — in South Africa, where the British fought the Boers. During the First World War, men from many countries died amongst the barbed-wire entanglements on the front lines. Today, barbed-wire fences guard the frontiers of some countries, or keep citizens out of areas governments wish to keep secret.

There is a Barbed Wire Museum at Canyon, Texas, with over two hundred different kinds of barbed wire in it. Some people collect barbed-wire specimens as enthusiastically as others collect stamps, and pay a lot for rare and rusty specimens.

Berlin Wall

CEMENT AND CONCRETE

Cement and concrete are very ancient materials. We do not know when people first found out that burnt lime, or burnt gypsum, mixed with water, set hard into a cement. Egyptian builders used gypsum cement four and a half thousand years ago. Cement was really a kind of paste which could be used to bind together stones or bricks and so build walls. Often sand was added to thin out the expensive cement. When other substances, such as gravel, or lumps of broken pottery or brick were added, the mixture was called concrete. Carefully and thoroughly stirred so that the cement and water coated everything in the mixture, concrete set as hard as natural stone.

The Romans discovered that if they added a fine, chocolate-red volcanic earth called *pozzolana* to lime, it made an extremely useful cement which set under water and was fire-resistant. Concrete made from this cement became a common building material in Imperial Rome, especially for large important buildings. The Romans' marvellous feats of construction with concrete were not equalled again until the industrial revolution forced men to rethink techniques of building. For, although cement and concrete are such ancient materials, they are also very modern. The trouble was no one really understood why cement worked. People left its making and mixing to trial and error. Sometimes medieval builders found their cement good and strong, at other times it crumbled disastrously. In fact, the chemical reactions involved in the making and setting of cement are most complicated and have only recently been understood.

Once men began to study the whys and hows of cement and concrete, new developments and important inventions came about that have made these materials indispensable to today's construction industry. Cement and concrete have almost unlimited uses, and engineers, architects and designers keep extending their possibilities. Highways, bridges, dams, skyscrapers — the new shapes of architecture and engineering — all come from modern uses of these ancient materials.

About two hundred years ago John Smeaton was given the job of rebuilding the Eddystone lighthouse in the English Channel. Smeaton decided he needed the best cement available to stand up to the pounding of the seas, so he collected samples of limestone from all over the country, tested them for strength and chemically analysed them. Smeaton discovered that limestone containing a lot of clay

Building of a town, using
mortar to bind bricks,
taken from mid 15th
century manuscript

made the most waterproof cement. Many new cements
were developed from his research. The best-known was
Roman cement, so called because people thought it made
concrete as hard as the concrete in buildings left over from
the Roman occupation of Britain.

In 1824 an important cement was patented by a Yorkshire
builder called Joseph Aspdin. Instead of trying to find
a clayey limestone as Smeaton had, Aspdin collected clay
from one place, limestone from another, ground them,
heated them to a very high temperature in a kiln, and re-
ground the resulting hard-burnt clinker into a powder.
Aspdin called his invention Portland cement, because he
wanted to suggest that its dull-grey colour resembled the
famous Portland stone used in many London buildings.
Portland cement might then be used to replace Portland
stone. Aspdin's son William started to manufacture the
cement on a large scale. Portland cement became the most
important modern cement, exported all over the world. It
got a real testing when the Metropolitan Board of Works
decided to use it in the middle of last century to build
London's drainage system, a job which took seventeen years.

53

Proper sewers and drains for cities were part of the needs of the fast-changing industrial society of the last century. With the great expansion of trade and manufacture, people and things had to be transported more efficiently. The old, unsealed road ending in a ford across a river was no longer good enough. Bridges must be built, as well as better roads, canals, tunnels, embankments for the new railways, and new harbour facilities — breakwaters, docks, quays — for more ships. All this meant reliable, high-quality cement and concrete capable of being used as a structural material in complex engineering works.

Concrete is immensely strong and can stand great direct pressure; it has compressive strength. But bend concrete and it cracks and breaks. It is not flexible; it does not have what is called tensile strength. In the middle of the last century several Frenchmen tried to get around this problem by embedding iron rods in concrete. A young French lawyer, Jean-Louis Lambot, and later a man called Joseph Monier made water containers and tubs for fruit-trees in this way. Some French builders had already tried laying wrought-iron rods in ceiling plaster to make it stronger, and an English builder, W. B. Wilkinson, tried reinforcing concrete beams with secondhand mining cable.

Monier took out a patent in 1867 for his reinforced concrete. His system worked because he used Portland cement, which was practically waterproof, and he made certain that a thick layer of concrete covered the reinforcing iron rods. In this way moisture could not creep through the concrete to rust the embedded iron and force the concrete apart. Gradually, designers and engineers began to use this revolutionary new material. Reinforced concrete had the compressive strength of concrete (it could withstand great direct pressure) married to the tensile strength of iron or steel (it was more flexible). But now the engineers needed to learn very precisely how steel and concrete worked together. In the early 1930s another Frenchman, Eugene Freyssinet, developed pre-stressed concrete. Steel wire was stretched while concrete was added, then allowed to set under pressure. The result was an even stronger, more flexible and resilient concrete. Pre-stressed concrete was particularly suitable for leaping, single-span bridges, domes on slender supports, and "floating" roofs.

About 1849 Jean-Louis Lambot decided to replace the

little wooden rowing-boat on the lake in his garden, because its timbers were rotting away. He built a boat of cement, reinforced with wire netting and iron bars. Then he built a better model, and the two boats floated on the lake under the hot sun of southern France for a hundred years, while children played in them. Lambot patented his techniques, but nothing came of them.

"Nothing floats like cement," claim the enthusiasts. A lump of cement or a bar of iron will sink to the bottom of the ocean. But combine them, and they can make a boat more satisfactory in many ways than a wooden one. That menace of ships, the marine borer, cannot worm its way into concrete, nor can rot and corrosion. A cement boat does not have to be hauled up regularly, scraped down and caulked as a wooden boat does. It is fireproof, and if it is holed it can easily be repaired. Most importantly, cement boats can be made much more easily and cheaply. The boatbuilders do not need to be as skilled, and the materials are always available. They are part of any building industry: sand, cement, wire mesh, steel or iron rod, tie wire and water.

In 1968 a United Nations boatbuilding expert was in Thailand designing and building a prototype cement boat for the Thai fishing industry. First, the skeleton of the boat was shaped out of ordinary water-piping and interwoven with a framework of flexible iron rods. Then wire mesh was tied onto the rods like a skin, four layers on the inside, four layers on the outside. Lastly, the cement mortar was added, a process rather like plastering. One man pushed it through the layers of mesh from the inside, making sure the cement filled all the spaces. A second man smoothed it off on the outside, watching that no bits of metal stuck through, and being careful that the cement covered the mesh evenly, and no thicker than $1/8$th of an inch. With this technique the cement layer covering the mesh must be very thin, or the surface will crack and break. The completed hull of the fifty-two-foot fishing vessel took about seventeen days to dry or "cure", although it would keep on increasing in strength over the years. Then the boat was painted, and superstructure such as engine, deckhouse and storage tanks added.

The ideas behind this technique are simple. The great Italian structural engineer Pier Luigi Nervi worked them out early in the Second World War, following on in many

Building of a concrete boat

In the south-west corner of the United States, Pueblo Indians used the simplest method for binding stones together: clayey earth mixed with water, which was called adobe. Later the Spaniards showed the Indians how to make bricks out of adobe mixed with chopped straw for added strength; they then dried hard in the sun.

ways from Jean-Louis Lambot's pioneer boat. Nervi found that if, instead of separate metal rods, soft iron wire mesh is used to reinforce concrete, extremely thin slabs can be cast into almost any shape and remain strong and highly flexible. The tensile strength of concrete is increased, the more the metal which reinforces it is divided up: this is why wire mesh is used. Nervi said the new material was like "melted stone"; he called it *ferrocemento*. Lambot had called his method *ferciment*. It is known today as ferro-cement; and an increasing number of ferro-cement boats are finding their way onto the world's lakes and oceans.

The massive unsupported domed ceiling of the Pantheon in Rome measures 142 feet across. It is made of concrete and brick, and no one has yet discovered exactly how it was constructed.

The "vertical railway"

Lifting appliance, about 1556

Touch the button for the thirty-fifth floor of a modern skyscraper, the elevator doors whoosh gently together, and you step out, four hundred feet up, thirty seconds later.

The ancestor of today's lift (or elevator as it is called in America) hoisted up beds exactly one floor in a New York factory a little over a hundred years ago. Men have known how to hoist weights up or down with pulleys and winches since ancient times. What made the lifting platform at the New York bedstead factory significant was a vital improvement designed by its builder, Elisha Graves Otis. A safety device automatically stopped the platform crashing down if the lifting rope broke.

Otis ran his own machine shop, doing odd jobs. He used the stream behind his house as a power source, but then the town took it over as part of the local water-supply, so Otis had to close down. He moved his family to New York, where he was put in charge of building a new bedstead factory. The factory needed a lift, and Otis invented one with the safety device.

Otis was thinking of joining the gold rush to California when he was asked to build two more of his 'safety hoisters'. With his two sons he opened a shop in part of the bedstead factory. Next year, in 1854, crowds at a New York exhibition watched a remarkable demonstration of Mr Otis's invention. Otis stood on the platform of his lift and had it

Elisha Graves Otis

hauled up to the highest point. With a flourish, the hoisting rope was cut. No crash to the death resulted; a smiling Otis stood on the platform held firm by its safety device. The lift was *safe* enough to carry *people*. Orders were still slow, so Otis manufactured several of his other inventions like a rotary baking oven.

Hotel owners were quick to see the advantages of lifts which could carry people safely. Now they could charge as much for rooms on the top floor as on the first floor — perhaps even more, if there was a view! The first practical passenger lift was installed in a New York hotel in 1859. It went up and down on a giant screw, and foreign visitors marvelled at this latest American gadget, although many hotel guests felt happier using the stairs. The first office block was equipped with a lift in 1868, and the top floor was immediately let at a large profit. Business and office buildings in big American cities now leapt up from five stories (which were all the stairs most people could manage) to eight, ten or even twelve stories. More people could now fit into the same ground space, so the value of building sites rose, and more people crowded into the cities.

Lift manufacturers kept busy improving the design and safety of the "vertical railway". Otis's two sons patented over thirty improvements to their father's invention. Hand-powered lifts quickly gave way to steam power, then hydraulics. In 1884 the first electric lift was installed. And in 1889 an Otis lift carried visitors up the 984 feet of the steel Eiffel Tower, the marvel of the Paris Exhibition. The tower was nearly twice as high as any other building previously erected.

Otis demonstrates at a New York exhibition, 1854

Right:

Universal Hoisting Machine

SKYSCRAPERS

Skyscrapers are an American invention. For people all over the world skyscrapers *stand* for America. "How dare they build anything 102 stories high?" demanded visitors in 1930, as the Empire State Building went up in the centre of New York City, one story a day, using 10 million bricks, having 6,400 windows, and visible 50 miles out to sea. The Empire State is still one of the tallest buildings in the world. Thousands of people take the lifts to the observation platforms and peer straight down at the city and harbour below.

In the 1920s American business men raced each other to build daring, boastful, beautiful skyscrapers which would tell everyone who gazed up at them how successful and go-ahead their businesses were. The sixty-story Woolworth Building dazzled everybody. It went up in 1913, and had spires and ornaments modelled on the Gothic cathedrals of Europe. Real estate men put higher and higher buildings on small blocks of land, and the value of each piece of ground went up and up.

Skyscrapers were not the invention of any one man. But they could not have been built without the invention and development of the lift, and the skeleton frame.

In 1887 passers-by in the city of Chicago had a nasty shock. Bricklayers were *starting* to lay the bricks of a new building *half-way up*. It didn't make sense. Walls begin at the bottom, otherwise how else could buildings stand up? Ever since man began building, in stone, mud, wood or brick, walls had to be strong and thick enough to take the weight of floors and roof. The great cathedrals built in the Middle Ages, almost thirty stories high some of them, had arms crooked out from the sides of the walls, called flying buttresses, to help take the strain. Castle walls were often fifteen feet thick at ground-floor level.

But the architects of the Chicago building whose walls began half-way up were using a new method to give it the strength to stand. The building had a skeleton of iron and steel bars, riveted firmly together. The walls were "hung", like curtains or clothes, to give privacy and protection from the weather, but not to hold the building up. The frame of iron and steel carried the weight of the building, which, in turn, was borne by the foundations. In one way the new building was like an Indian tepee: a strong frame of poles tied firmly together, with the buffalo hide hung and stretched over it for protection from the weather. The same principle applies to our bodies; it is the skeleton that holds us up, not the outside wall of skin.

An architect called Major William LeBaron Jenney probably made the first building using a skeleton frame, in Chicago, in 1883. He was asked to design a fireproof office building with as much light and space inside as possible. He reckoned that a box of cast-iron columns and steel beams would take all the weight of the structure and leave the walls free for big windows. He hung the floors from the iron frame too.

Buildings stayed around five stories high as long as people had to climb stairs. But with a lift, you could start scraping the clouds! Builders quickly found out, however, that buildings with more than about ten stories had such thick walls at ground level they took up too much valuable floor space.

A few adventurous and inventive architects tried to forget the age-old method of building. They wanted to use different materials and develop new techniques for this problem of building tall. Engineers became as important as architects in solving the problems. Whole new methods of construction were worked out which were later applied to the construction and building industry generally. Ways of making foundations were borrowed from bridge builders. Prefabrication of parts such as steel girders, concrete wall slabs, and floor sections began, and heavy complex machinery was designed to lift and carry huge weights.

London's first high building, and the last for eighty years, was put up in the early 1880s. It was a fourteen-story-high block of flats, called Queen Anne's Mansions, in brown brick. Queen Victoria could see its rather ugly back from Buckingham Palace and she didn't like it. Immediately a wave of new laws, about such things as fire regulations, made it quite unprofitable to construct any more high buildings in London.

Much the same sort of thing happened in other European cities. A skyscraper is a problem in old, traditional, beautiful places. It looks so different, perched high in the sky, changing a familiar skyline, peering down into private courtyards and gardens. City planners thought long and hard before the first skyscrapers began to be built in London, Milan, Berlin, Paris, in the 1950s. Many people complain bitterly about the skyscraper invasion. Others

New York

Sydney

see the tall buildings as signs of progress. Americans call them pocket skyscrapers, because they are usually only thirty to fifty stories high.

Today's skyscrapers are steel-and-glass blocks turned on end. They look pretty much alike wherever they appear in the world, and very different from the original skyscrapers with their towers and spires and carving. The straight, wide tops of the new skyscrapers being built in New York are blocking out the old famous skyline of early skyscrapers.

The New Yorker who travelled rather nervously down the lift in a skyscraper at the beginning of this century wasn't making much of a journey compared with the distance a gold-miner at Bendigo, in Australia, travelled every day to work. The shafts of these "skyscrapers in reverse" went down 2,000 feet, then fanned out into tunnels. The reasons for making them deep were rather the same as the reasons for building tall in New York. Most of the mining companies could only claim a small area of ground to mine, so they had to keep going down to get the gold. Skyscraper builders in New York went up in the air to get a different kind of gold from their small plots of land.

DYNAMITE

"If I have a thousand ideas a year and only one turns out to be good, I'm satisfied"

DYNAMITE OR NOBEL'S SAFETY BLASTING POWDER. It was one of those inventions people seemed to have been waiting for. Alfred Nobel had to waste no time persuading people to try his product. Men were greedy to use this new violent power, to get hold of this explosive which could blow up mountains and tunnel out mines. In fact, Nobel had to spend his time trying to stop people from making and selling dynamite without paying him royalties on his patents. In the end he managed to keep most of the manufacture of his inventions under his own control, and as a result he became an extremely rich, international tycoon, with factories all over the world. Explosives very quickly became vital commodities both to industry and to war.

Nowadays, high explosives mean military weapons to most of us. Alfred Nobel always said that he did not want the explosives he invented to be used for war, "the horror of horrors and the greatest of all crimes". They were needed for peaceful jobs in mining, industry and transport, to build roads and railways, quarry metals and blast mountains. The great engineering projects of the last hundred years would have been impossible without dynamite. But governments quickly saw the war potential of a really powerful explosive, and military engineers designed devastating new weapons using dynamite. And Nobel himself became very interested in the technical side of fire-arms, inventing and patenting many improvements.

Alfred Nobel lived a life full of contrasts. He was shy, lonely and hated publicity, yet dynamite is one of the most familiar patented names in the world. He always thought of himself as a Swede, although he only lived in Sweden until he was nine years old, returning for brief periods. He was a sickly child, with very little schooling, and a frail man. Yet he worked himself unbelievably hard, and was a great inventor and industrialist as well as being widely read and fluent in five languages. He wanted to be an inventor all the time, and his happiest days were spent in his laboratory experimenting. Yet he quickly became a powerful international financier continually involved in law suits and business problems. He was an idealist, yet he has been condemned as the inventor of great destructive forces.

Nobel had an extraordinary father, Immanuel, who was always working on inventions and schemes to make money. These often failed, which left the family very poor. When Alfred was nine, his father summoned the family to Russia,

The use of explosives, from a Byzantine manuscript

Manufacture of
cannon, 16th century

to St Petersburg, where he had set up a factory making
military weapons, machine tools, and central-heating pipes.
Immanuel Nobel's factory was very important in starting
the Russia of the Czars on its industrial revolution. But
after some years a new Czar closed the factory, though
Alfred's two elder brothers stayed on and eventually
founded Russia's huge oil industry. Alfred did his first
experimenting with explosives in St Petersburg.

In 1846, when Alfred Nobel was thirteen, an Italian
chemist called Ascanio Sobrero made an explosive so
dangerous he begged everyone to forget about it. Sobrero
added glycerine to nitric and sulphuric acids, then poured
the compound into a basin of water. The pale-yellow oil
which sank to the bottom was called nitroglycerine. It was
not detonated by a spark or flame, like gunpowder, but by
impact — percussion. Drop a small bottle of nitroglycerine
in the laboratory, and the whole building would be blown
sky-high.

Alfred became fascinated by this sensitive, risky, but
extraordinarily powerful, new oil. For centuries the only
available explosive had been gunpowder, which was useful
but limited. Alfred and his father were now back in Sweden,
and both began experimenting with nitroglycerine, separately. Explosives are useful only when they are controlled.
Alfred Nobel was determined to find a way to control the
detonation of nitroglycerine — the size and the timing of

the explosion. In 1863 he invented the blasting cap, which effectively detonated nitroglycerine by means of a small explosion of gunpowder. It was a new and vital technique in the science of explosives.

Alfred was now certain that nitroglycerine had an enormous future. But the public was most suspicious about the explosive. After a lot of trouble, Nobel was given permission to start manufacturing nitroglycerine with the blasting cap — he called it Nobel's Blasting Oil — on board a barge moored in the middle of a Swedish lake. Then, in 1864, a terrible explosion destroyed the Nobels' experimental workshop in the garden of their home, killing, among others, Alfred's younger brother, and shattering his father's health. The situation was critical. Reports kept coming in of appalling accidents. People so often just did not realize how the slightest shock, or even change in temperature, could cause the risky oil to explode. There were dreadful difficulties in transporting it, particularly overland, or round the coast to California where gold-miners wanted to get their hands on the explosive at any cost. Hair-raising stories were told of people using nitroglycerine for lamp oil, boot polish, or for greasing wagon wheels — the sort of mistake that a person could only make once. The factory that Nobel established in Germany was twice destroyed by explosion in less than five years.

A way had to be found of making nitroglycerine less dangerous, safer to transport, yet as powerful. In 1864 Nobel decided to try using *kieselguhr,* a very porous kind of earth found in certain places: for example, in northern Germany. He discovered that it soaked up the nitroglycerine without changing its chemical composition; the resulting mixture could be made into hard cakes or sticks. Here was the answer. Nobel patented his invention in 1867, and called the new explosive "dynamite" (after the Greek word *dynamis* meaning power). Dynamite was really nitroglycerine, tamed.

Now Nobel hurried to patent this invention in major European countries, to get it made in his factories, and organize ways of transporting it wherever it was needed. It was a restless, nerve-racking life. Some governments, frightened by nitroglycerine's power, and prodded by public horror at explosion accidents, refused to allow it to be imported into their countries. The big gunpowder manufacturers tried to stop it. The French government

At the same time as William the Conqueror landed in England and attacked the English armies with bow and arrow, and sword, Chinese generals had sophisticated flame-throwing machines using gunpowder.

would not let Nobel build a dynamite factory in France, until war with Germany in 1870 forced them to insist on it in a hurry. German sappers used the new explosive to blow up age-old French forts and bridges. In Great Britain, after restrictions and delays, Nobel built his dynamite factory on the lonely west coast of Scotland, at Ardeer. For twenty years all railways in England refused to carry nitroglycerine explosives. So Nobel had to arrange for transport by horse and cart. Later the company organized its own fleet of specially built steamers. In the United States, Nobel found competition from unscrupulous business men determined to get in on the profitable explosives trade so distasteful that he swore never to return. Vigorite, Rendrock, Hercules, Railroad-Powder appeared on the market in America — explosives made to Nobel's formula with tiny changes.

Despite all the official restrictions, everyone wanted to use Nobel's explosives. Within six years of patenting dynamite, Nobel had sixteen factories in twelve different countries. At the time of his death, a little over twenty years later, ninety-three factories all over the world produced 66,500 tons of dynamite a year. Ninety years after dynamite was patented, over 400,000 tons were produced annually in the United States alone. So the business grew, gathering allied concerns into huge new industrial groupings. They learnt to co-operate internationally and not compete — until wars came and governments took over arms manufacture. Then Nobel factories literally hurled destruction at one another, each making explosives based on the same Nobel patents. The German factory was destroyed for the last time in April 1945, wiped out by over a thousand heavy bombs whose explosive power was based on Alfred's own inventions. In Great Britain, Nobel Industries eventually joined with other companies to become the huge Imperial Chemical Industries (I.C.I.).

Nobel went on experimenting with explosives for the rest of his life. In 1875 he created an important new explosive, a jelly-like mixture of gun cotton and nitro-glycerine called blasting gelatin. It was more powerful than dynamite, almost insensitive to shock, and could be detonated under water. Nobel built a slender steel jetty out into the Mediterranean from his beautiful Italian villa and tested his explosives and fire-arms from the end of it. His wealthy neighbours in their beautiful villas were not at all pleased.

But Nobel was interested in all kinds of things besides explosives: synthetic rubber, blood transfusions, improvements to the telephone, aerial photography. "I'm going to send up a little balloon with a parachute, a camera, and a small clockwork or time fuse," he wrote just before his death. "At a suitable altitude the balloon will be automatically deflated or separated from the parachute, which will then come down with the picture in the camera." "If I have a thousand ideas a year," he said, "and only one turns out to be good, I'm satisfied." As an old man visiting Sweden, Nobel used to spend the little leisure time he allowed himself being driven in a small light carriage drawn by two stallions. Passers-by would see the shy man, wrapped in a fur coat, taking notes by electric light run off special accumulators. He had a telephone to the coachman, and rubber bands fastened around the carriage wheels to cut down unnecessary noise — the explosives man's special hate. During his last illness Nobel was ordered to take nitroglycerine. It had been developed as a medicine. "They call it Trinitrin, so as not to scare pharmacists and public," said Nobel.

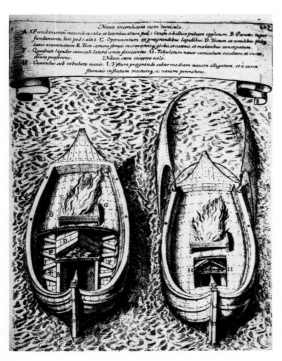

The use of gunpowder led to the invention of the cannon, and later all types of hand-gun. Until the middle of the last century, gunpowder was the only important explosive men knew about.

A fireship, forerunner of the torpedo

Nobel died in 1896. He left a four-page will, made the year before at his Paris home, written in Swedish. It was a remarkable will:

The capital . . . shall constitute a fund, the interest of which shall be annually distributed in the form of prizes to those who, during the preceding year, shall have conferred the greatest benefit on mankind. The said interest shall be divided into five equal parts, which shall be apportioned as follows: one part to the person who shall have made the most important discovery or invention within the field of physics; one part to the person who shall have made the most important chemical discovery or improvement; one part to the person who shall have made the most important discovery within the domain of physiology or medicine; one part to the person who shall have produced in the field of literature the most outstanding work of an idealist tendency; and one part to the person who shall have done the most or the best work to promote fraternity between nations, for the abolition or reduction of standing armies and for the holding and promotion of peace congresses. . . . It is my express wish that in awarding the prizes no consideration whatever shall be given to the nationality of the candidates, but the most worthy shall receive the prize, whether he be a Scandinavian or not.

There was a terrible fight over Nobel's will. What did it mean? How could it be carried out? The newspapers were very critical — the will should be declared invalid. How unpatriotic of Nobel to ignore Swedish interests in favour of international activity. It would cause nothing but trouble and quarrelling. But several devoted friends worked hard untangling all the legal, financial and political problems, trying to interpret Nobel's wishes. The Nobel Foundation was set up in 1900, and the first awards were made the next year.

Nobel Prizes today are perhaps the most valued prizes in the world. They are distributed in a solemn ceremony every year on 10th December, the anniversary of Nobel's death. Alfred Nobel's name stands for much more than dynamite.

THE VACUUM CLEANER

H. Cecil Booth went with a friend to the Empire Music Hall in London to see an American inventor demonstrate his new dust-removing machine. It was a box, with a bag on top supplied with compressed air. The air blew down into a carpet and made the dust blow up into the box. Booth didn't think much of the idea: a lot of the dust went either side of the box and just settled back on the carpet. "Why don't you *suck* out the dust?" Booth asked the inventor, who became very angry. "It's not possible, and in any case it's been tried over and over again and no one has succeeded," he told Booth. Booth thought about this for several days, then, as he said later, "I tried the experiment of sucking with my mouth against the back of a plush seat in a restaurant in Victoria Street." So much dust came out he almost choked. "I came to the conclusion," he said, "that I could construct a machine to work by suction."

The machine Booth designed and patented in 1901 was so large that it sat on a trolley and had to be pulled along the street. There was a pump, a dust filter, and the power unit. One attendant worked the machine while another guided a long flexible hose inside offices or houses to clean them. Booth made sure his pump created enough of a vacuum to suck out the dust embedded in and trapped underneath carpets and upholstery. Booth called his machine a vacuum cleaner. He was not in fact the inventor of the suction dust-removal machine, although at the time he did not know any of the details of the previous attempts to make a cleaner based on this method. No one has really agreed who invented the modern type of vacuum cleaner. The two earliest, called carpet sweepers, were invented in 1859 and 1860. Although nothing came of these inventions, they turned out to be the prototypes of the two main designs used today. One relied on suction alone, the other used suction plus brushes to loosen the dirt.

Vacuum cleaners on little trucks like Booth's were also invented and used in France. The Americans were the first to develop very large suction machines — a sort of central cleaning system — which were installed in the basements of buildings such as theatres, hotels and department stores. In England, Booth put one in the House of Commons. Pipes led up to outlet points for attachments which sucked dust down into containers. Before the First World War, smaller versions of these stationary machines were popular

"I tried the experiment of sucking with my mouth against the back of a plush seat in a restaurant"

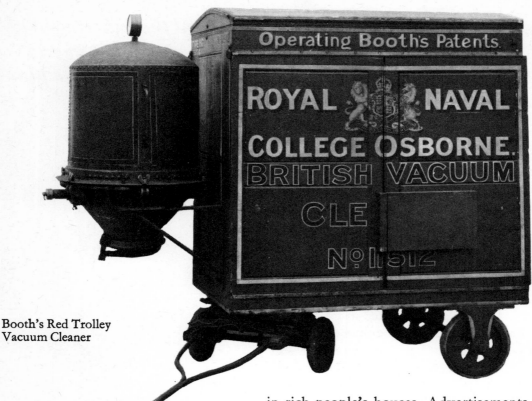

Booth's Red Trolley
Vacuum Cleaner

in rich people's houses. Advertisements showed the lady's maid using an attachment plugged into the wall to clean her mistress's hat, a servant downstairs dusting his master's coat, while other servants cleaned furniture and carpets all over the house.

But inventors were keen to develop a handy portable vacuum cleaner for home use. One of the first was patented in America as early as 1908; it was called the Electrical Vacuum Carpet Sweeper. It was made by a poor, sick, unsuccessful inventor called James Murray Spangler, who had been reduced to caretaking an office. He saw one of the huge stationary machines at work and thought up a small machine with a revolving brush to loosen the dirt, and suction to remove it. William Henry Hoover, who ran a tanning factory in Ohio, bought the rights to manufacture the machine, but Spangler died before the Hoover became famous.

The vacuum in some of the early portable machines was made by working a bellows up and down by hand. But it was the development of the small electric motor which really put the convenient home vacuum cleaner on the market.

It took a little while for people to realize the advantages of using a vacuum cleaner. They were too used to the dreadful drudgery of cleaning with dusters, brushes, and by carpet beating. Spring cleaning was a yearly horror. "It completely upset the household routine and comfort for weeks," said H. Cecil Booth. All through the winter, mess from fires added to the general dust in a house. Spring sunshine revealed the grimy layers; so everything was covered, moved, beaten and shaken. But a lot of dust just settled back down again. There was no cleaning aid that could really get inside heavy curtain materials, carpets and upholstered chairs to dislodge the years of ingrained dirt.

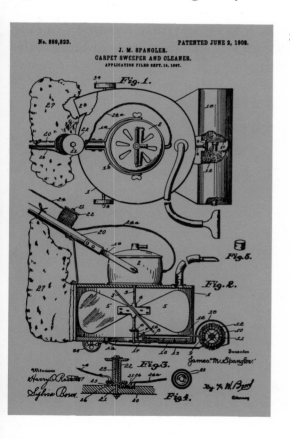

Spangler's patent 1908

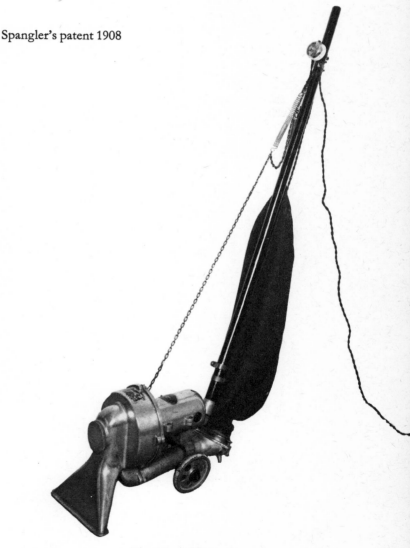

The Magic Vacuum
Cleaner

Sanitation and health were greatly improved by the introduction of the vacuum cleaner. Tons of germ-laden dust were moved for the first time from theatre seats and shop floors. One of the first jobs for Booth's original machine was to clean the great blue coronation carpet in Westminster Abbey before Edward VII's coronation ceremony. During the First World War, Booth received an emergency call to take his machines to the Crystal Palace — that famous relic of London's Great 1851 Exhibition. Naval Reserve men quartered inside the building were falling sick and dying from spotted fever. For two weeks, fifteen of Booth's machines sucked up inches of dust from the floors and girders, walls and staircases of the old building. Twenty-six tons of dust were removed from the Crystal Palace and buried, and that was the end of the spotted-fever epidemic.

Earliest of the Hoover cleaners

PASTEURIZED MILK

Microbes are everywhere. Tiny living organisms, feeding, multiplying, in the air, the soil, on our hands, in food, in our intestines. They maintain the cycle of life, growth and decay. Microbes are the microscopic creatures for which we have many names: we call them germs, moulds, yeasts, bacteria, viruses. One thousand bacteria laid end to end would cross the head of a pin. In every gram of fertile soil there exist about one hundred million living bacteria. Most of these teeming microbe populations are harmless. Many are very useful, but some can cause disease in men, animals and plants.

Anton van Leeuwenhoek, a Dutchman, was the first to learn of the existence of microbes; he saw some squirming and multiplying under the newly invented microscope in 1674. Leeuwenhoek spat on a glass plate and looked in astonishment at this new world of living creatures that inhabited his mouth. But until the middle of last century men knew almost nothing about microbes or what they did. The fact that we eat, sleep, live and breathe microbes has only been realized during the last hundred years or so. Most of modern medicine and hygiene depends on understanding the existence and role of microbes. The man who did most towards this understanding was the great French chemist Louis Pasteur.

"How explain the disintegration of a dead body or a fallen plant?" asked Pasteur. "How account for the working of the vintage in the vat? Of dough left to rise and then souring? Of curdling milk? Of straw ripening on the dungheap? Of dead leaves and plants buried in the soil and turning to humus?" Accepted theories were most confused. Some leading scientists thought these changes were chemical, that they were caused perhaps by the oxygen in the air. Many scientists believed in something called spontaneous combustion: that some things just sprang into life, that maggots, for example, were "made" by putrid meat. Pasteur's research and thinking and experiments made him decide that all living things can come only from other living things. And that changes like decay and fermentation (which he investigated carefully in the making of beer and wine) were caused by living things — microbes — and not by chemical reactions, as other scientists thought. Pasteur was only thirty-four when he published an important paper in 1857 putting forward these theories.

Pasteur realized that some microbes perform useful tasks

One thousand bacteria laid end to end would cross the head of a pin

which could be interrupted by other harmful microbes. From this, he and other scientists began to understand how microbes can cause different infections and diseases, and therefore how to begin to combat them. Antiseptics and disinfectants began to be used in medicine with real under-standing to control infection. A few doctors — and this was only a hundred years ago — had already realized that dirty hands and dirty clothes spread infection, but had not known why. They were laughed at and criticized for their stupid ideas. How could a dirty shirt-sleeve have an invisible, living, disease-carrying agent on it? By the mid-nineteenth century, some people knew that water polluted by sewage and the muck of towns could carry diseases like the cholera that swept England in four epi-demics after 1830, killing about one hundred thousand people. But they didn't know what it was in the water that did this. In 1861 Queen Victoria's beloved husband, Prince Albert, fell sick of typhoid fever, probably contracted from contaminated water. All that the best doctors could do was diagnose a "slow fever", feel his brow, advise him to rest, and wait while the illness "took its course" . . . and the Prince Consort died, aged forty-four.

Milk, that great all-in-one food for humans, turned out to be an excellent food for bacteria. Disease-carrying bacteria could get in any time during handling of the milk from cow to customer. Some bacteria which could infect humans came straight from diseases in the cow itself, such as the dangerous and common bovine tuberculosis. Pasteur's researches showed that heating a liquid food to a certain temperature kills most of the harmful bacteria present. The process came to be called pasteurization. But it took a long time to be applied to milk.

Getting milk from the cow to the customer before it spoils has always been a problem. Milk lasts only if it is turned into butter or cheese. As long as towns stayed fairly small, cows could be kept close enough to people's houses for the milk to be delivered while it was still fresh. Some-times (and this still happens in parts of the world) the cow was walked from house to house and milked straight into a container provided by the customer. Or open carts carried milk through the streets, and people bought what they needed. There were plenty of chances for dirty handling and bacterial infection. Cows kept in New York City were fed on such poor food they gave no cream. When the first

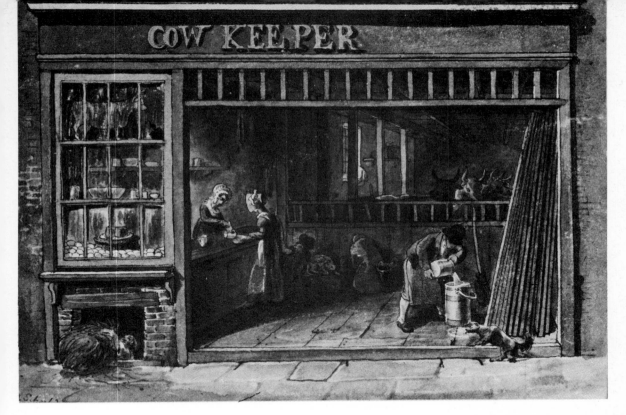

trains brought milk in from the country in 1842, people complained. What was this yellow scum on top of their milk?

Towards the end of the nineteenth century German researchers gathered evidence about the bacteria in milk which were harmful to humans, and the German Emperor insisted that commercial dairies pasteurize their milk. It was already being done in Denmark. But the idea of pasteurization did not really catch on. People did not like their milk being messed around with, or drinking what they called "dead bodies" in it. As early as 1886 a German chemist had advised mothers to feed babies with sterilized milk in sterilized bottles, but that was not popular either.

In the 1890s a German immigrant to New York who had made lots of money went home to the old country, where he heard about pasteurization. He came back to New York and opened a milk kitchen in a poor area of the city where he had once lived, giving free pasteurized milk to anyone who came. Hardly anyone did. But the man would not give up. With the help of a biologist from the university, he decided to conduct an experiment. Everyone in one row of streets was persuaded to get their milk from his free kitchen. Everyone in the next row bought theirs as usual from milk sellers in the streets. A careful count of the

An 18th Century town dairy

75

cases of scarlet fever and diphtheria in the two areas was kept. The results were such startling proof of the value of pasteurization in cutting down disease that New York City soon passed a law requiring pasteurization in all commercial dairies.

But arguments and prejudice still continued. Some people were convinced that pasteurization was harmful, or wasn't necessary. Why interfere with cows' milk? Careful research and scientific proof made no difference, once people had made up their minds. Certainly, improved methods of dairying and milk handling greatly reduced the risk of bacterial infection. Pasteurization became much more accepted and widespread in England during the Second World War, and today almost all milk there is treated.

The exact temperature for pasteurization varies from country to country. Generally it means heating milk to between 61° and 63° centigrade for thirty minutes, or 71° to 72° centigrade for fifteen seconds. The taste does not change, no nutritional value is lost, and the milk is now quite safe to drink. It also lasts much longer because many of the bacteria which turn milk sour are killed. Pasteurization is not a complicated process. But it must be carefully controlled, and of course it is no use if bacteria are allowed to infect the milk again afterwards through careless handling.

In 1824 a four-pound tin of roast veal made the long voyage to the Arctic Circle and back. It was part of the stores taken by Sir William Edward Parry on his expedition to search for a north-west passage through the ice around the top of America. The veal wasn't needed, so two years later the same tin went on Parry's next voyage of discovery. Still it wasn't eaten. "ROASTED VEAL, *cut round on the top near to the outer edge with a chisel and hammer*," read the instructions on the side of the container. Somehow it got stored at a military museum. Here it stayed until 1938, when excited scientists prepared to open the oldest known tin of preserved meat. What would the veal cooked a hundred and fourteen years ago be like? The tin had survived all its travels without denting or perforating. And the big pieces of pink veal inside were in perfect condition. They looked as if they had been recently cooked. Laboratory mice and a cat fed portions of Admiral Parry's roast veal enjoyed every bit.

In 1824 the canning of foods was a new process. A Frenchman, Nicolas Appert, worked out the methods in the small kitchen behind his shop in a village near Paris. Appert had trained as a chef, brewer and confectioner, all useful qualifications in his search for a new way of preserving foods. He began experimenting in 1795. France was in a turmoil of revolution and war. The Emperor Napoleon led his armies through Europe — and marching armies needed food above all. Napoleon offered a prize of twelve thousand francs to the inventor of a new process for preserving food.

Like everyone else, Appert thought that contact with the air, probably the oxygen in it, caused food to decay and spoil. So he packed food into glass containers, specially designed with wide tops. The bottles were loosely corked, heated in a water bath while air was driven off, then tightly corked so no more air could enter, and boiled again. This method is in fact almost the same as people use today to preserve fruit and vegetables at home. By 1804 he had carried out hundreds of experiments to discover how much heating for how long was best for which kinds of meat, vegetables, fruit, even milk. Often he had to wait months, watching to see if the bottled food would after all go bad. In 1810 Appert published his book *The Art of Preserving All Kinds of Animal and Vegetable Substances for Several Years*. He described how to preserve the simplest foods, as well as the most elaborate, such as: "A matelot of eels, carp and pike, with veal sweetbreads, mushrooms and anchovy

"*Cut round on the top near to the outer edge with a chisel and hammer*"

Can of roast veal taken on Parry's voyage to the Arctic in 1824.

Nicolas Appert
(1750-1840): "My method
is no mere theory; it is the
fruit of my dreams, of my
reflections, of my
researches, and of
countless experiments."

Stoves and autoclaves for
processing canned foods,
France, 1860 or later

butter, the whole cooked in white wine." Appert won Napoleon's prize and invested all the money in more experiments and a food-processing factory. He died poor, but his descendants ran a successful business for many years.

In England, Peter Durand read the translation of Nicolas Appert's book. He decided that tin plate would make a much better container for preserved foods than glass. It was stronger, lighter, conducted heat better, could be formed into any shape, and completely sealed. Tin plate — rolled iron with a minute layer of tin — had been made in Britain since the early eighteenth century, using tin mined in Cornwall. The owners of an iron works in London, John Hall and Bryan Donkin, saw the opportunity for business. They experimented with the temperatures and times needed to preserve foods in the new tinned canisters, and by 1812 were able to offer their revolutionary product to the British Admiralty. Ships' rations had been salt meat and hard biscuit for hundreds of years. The naval authorities knew that sailors died of the dreaded scurvy because they lacked fresh vegetables and fruit. Here was the chance to change shipboard diet. Tinned vegetable soups, carrots, meat: all were tried on long sea voyages, at lonely outposts and on expeditions like Parry's. They proved successful. Donkin and Hall had a special method of checking their products. After cooking, stacks of containers were put in a test chamber, with temperatures around 100° Fahrenheit for a month. If the food were eventually to go bad, it did so now: the ends of the tins bulged with gases and sometimes exploded. If they survived this treatment they would survive anything, boasted the manufacturers. "Meat thus preserved eats nothing, nor drinks — it is not apt to die — does not tumble overboard," wrote a delighted naval officer. "It is always ready, may be eaten hot or cold. . . ."

Several Englishmen took the newly invented method of preserving food to America in 1817. William Underwood carried out his preserving of fruit and pickles in New York, but carefully labelled the bottles "Canned in Britain" so that they would sell better. Tin cans were not used in America until 1840. The Civil War in the 1860s increased production tremendously: food for the troops again. All Gail Borden's newly invented condensed milk in cans was commandeered by the Northern army. About a hundred years ago the enormous meat-packing industries using

Sir Joseph Banks, President of the Royal Society, to Donkin and Hall, Blue Anchor Road, Bermondsey, Southwark, 1814: *I know of no objection to my name being placed among the very respectable names which are printed in your Prospectus, as giving their testimony in favour of the nutritious qualities of your embalmed Provisions.*

canning techniques were started in Chicago. Australia was ahead of the United States in the canning business. Two wealthy grazier brothers opened the first factory in New South Wales in 1847; and soon canned mutton was being exported to England.

About the middle of last century, scandals broke out in England. The meat in tins was bad! Thousands of containers were condemned as unfit for human consumption. One big English firm had a factory in Rumania; the angry British public accused this firm of putting old, unhealthy animals into tins. The trouble was that no one really understood the processes of food preservation. *Why* did Appert's methods of heating and air removal usually work? In the 1850s, research by the French chemist Louis Pasteur revealed the part microbes play in the decomposition of food. He showed the importance of heat in killing the polluting microbes, and the need to keep food from all contact with the air immediately after heating. But Pasteur's researches were not used in the canning industry for another forty years. Canners worked by trial and error, and losses from spoiling were often heavy.

Part of the trouble was that manufacturers around 1850 began to save time and space by preserving food in much bigger containers. An old man interviewed when the roasted veal tin was opened in 1938 said he had once talked to an Admiralty inspector who checked bad tins in 1850: the meat in the centre of each tin was quite uncooked: the cans were too big for heat to penetrate right through, so sterilization could not take place.

Manufacturers had developed methods of heating containers to temperatures higher than the boiling point of water by using calcium chloride, or by primitive forms of pressure cookers or autoclaves. But the troubles continued. For years people tried to find ways of lacquering the inside of tins to deal with another problem: the discoloration and

tainting that occurred in certain foods. In the 1890s, in America, the first real research on canning was carried out, and the scientific control of canning began, slowly. It took time, and often special laws, to convince manufacturers that scientists could tell them anything useful. The food industry was full of 'secret' methods with little outside supervision or control. But, gradually, the bacteria which caused decomposition were identified. Manufacturers found that to guarantee safety they had to work out a schedule of handling, temperature and time for each different food they wanted to put into cans. But the public took many years to forget the mistakes of the past.

Some foods needed to be canned as quickly as possible, and factories were set up near farms. Mass-production began to come in, particularly in the United States. Each tin can was made by hand even as late as the 1860s, and the tops sealed on by soldering. Now machines were invented to cut, shape and seal cans automatically. As a result, new machinery was needed to harvest and prepare crops fast enough to fill the waiting cans. Mechanical pea-pickers snapped up whole plants (special varieties were developed to ripen at the same time) and a single shelling machine removed peas from pods as fast as six hundred hand workers could shell them. One of the new corn-cutting machines in the 1890s could strip enough ears in one day to pack fifteen hundred cans. The Chinese did all the work in the salmon-canning factories on the west coast of America until they were excluded from the country in the 1890s. So the Iron Chink was invented, a machine that adjusted itself to the size of each fish, gutted it, removed head, tail and fins, and chopped it ready for canning. All in less than one second.

Plants and animals start decaying after they stop living. Man's problem from the beginning was how to delay that decay, so that he could have enough to eat — when winter

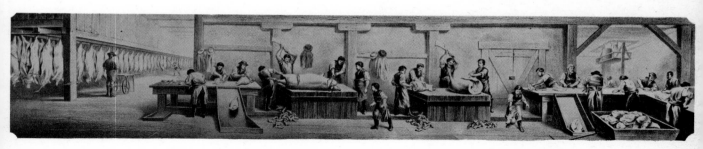

came and nothing grew, when the herds moved away and he couldn't hunt for food, when he was sick and couldn't go out to find it. Some ways of preserving food are immensely old: storing, drying, smoking, soaking in salt, chilling. Preserving in sugar, vinegar or spices were essential methods for our ancestors. Wars were fought, empires won and great journeys made to secure rich spices. Spices, as well as preserving food, hid the taste when it had gone bad. Age-old routes crossed continents to the sources of salt. Indians on the great American plains dried slices of buffalo meat and ground them into powder which they mixed with dried berries and melted fat to form hard cakes known as pemmican. It was food for the trail, easily carried, which wouldn't decay. Captain Cook took small hard cakes of "portable soup" on his great voyage around the world in 1772–75. They looked like hard glue and were probably made of meat and bones boiled down and dried; mixed with flour and water, they helped sick sailors suffering from the inadequate diet of salt meat and biscuit. Dried foods — powdered potato, carrots and meat — were sent to soldiers dying from scurvy in the Crimean War. They tasted horrible and were very unpopular, and had little food value left at all. Nicolas Appert's invention of a new method of preserving food was a revolution. Food could now last, and be taken anywhere. Canned foods took the drudgery out of cooking, the monotony out of meals, the hunger from campers, city dwellers, explorers, sailors, armies. Canned foods have made the world's food available the world over every day of the year.

Pork-packing, Chicago late 1860s. One of the first assembly lines— from hog to pork in $2\frac{1}{2}$ minutes.

Someone made a joke. "Why not collect the ice off our ponds and sell it in the tropics!" Everyone at the party laughed. They were all keen enough to make money, and there seemed plenty of ways to do it in the United States of America at the beginning of last century. But to take the ice from the ponds around their city of Boston during the freezing winter months, and try to ship it to the hot, steamy islands of the Caribbean! It would all melt away, taking their money with it! To twenty-one-year-old Frederick Tudor, however, it was an idea to work on. Before a year was up, in 1806, he shipped 130 tons of ice south from Boston, Massachusetts, to the tropical island of Martinique in the West Indies. Tudor became the "Ice King". By the 1840s clear, natural ice from the ponds of Massachusetts cooled drinks half a world away: in India, China, Australia, the Philippines.

Tudor spent years battling with the technical problems of how to stop ice melting. He built special "ice-houses" at the ports where his ships berthed, then experimented with ways of insulating them, using straw, wood shavings, even blankets. Watch in hand, he would stand outside each newly insulated house in the hot sun, measuring the rate at which the ice melted. He succeeded in designing a tropical

Boston sea captains braved the Labrador icebergs and chipped off big pieces to take south

KNICKERBOCKER C? CUTTING ICE.

ROCKLAND LAKE.

Published at the Office of the Knickerbocker Ice C? New York.

83

ice depot where only 8 per cent of the stored ice melted in a season. Tudor persuaded the local populations to enjoy iced drinks, ice-cream, chilled fruit, and all the other luxuries ice could bring. In winters when not enough ice formed on the ponds, Boston sea captains braved the Labrador icebergs and chipped off big pieces to take south. But these odd-shaped lumps of ice were difficult to stack and melted easily.

Tudor asked a friend to invent a machine which chopped the surface of a pond into neat ice cakes all the same size. Packed together with sawdust or straw, a heap of these blocks could last beside a pond for several years, like an untidy ice castle. Every winter, hundreds of labourers descended on the ponds to harvest the ice. Lucky Australian gold-diggers toasted their new wealth in Melbourne pubs with drinks cooled by Boston ice. A Persian prince sent Tudor a message of gratitude for ice which was saving the lives of patients in Persian hospitals: placed on the forehead it helped to lower fevers.

Farmers around the city of London in the 1830s used to flood their fields at the beginning of winter. Everyone helped to pile the first thin sheets of ice into carts, for delivery in the city. In the middle of November ice could fetch 15s. a cartload. Thousands of tons of ice were stored in a big underground ice-house where, with luck, some of it lasted all through the summer. It was used to keep the fish fresh on London fish stalls.

Ice is one of the oldest and best preservers of food. At low temperatures the bacteria which cause food to deteriorate are either destroyed or become almost inactive. But natural ice by itself is a very vulnerable refrigerator. Even in cold climates the weather can play tricks, unexpectedly melt the ice and spoil carefully stored food. Eighty years ago America suffered the "great ice famine". The warmest winter on record was followed by a hot summer. All the stored ice had melted by July, and the newspapers were filled with lurid stories of putrid meat, soured milk, and epidemics of typhus.

What was needed was a way to make ice artificially and cheaply, wherever and whenever anyone wanted it. Ice-making machines began to be designed and patented in the 1830s. One of the best was developed in Australia by the editor of the Geelong newspaper, James Harrison.

The big problem in Australia in the middle of last century

Ice store in Chelsea, 1861

was surplus meat. It wasn't practical to send sheep or cattle alive by ship to European markets. Canned meat wasn't very popular. Millions of Australian sheep were boiled down for tallow, which was shipped to England to make soap. At least the hungry English workman could wash his hands cheaply before he ate his expensive, locally produced mutton.

Harrison believed that ice was the answer. He remembered that, as a child in Scotland, he had seen his father and other fishermen using American pond ice to preserve their salmon catch. Harrison believed that if meat carcasses could be frozen they would last the long sea journey across the Equator to England, and arrive in good condition. In 1857, after several years' experimenting, he patented a process which produced the first synthetic ice in Australia. Experts agreed it was "much more complete and practical than any other process" so far invented.

The next problem was how to keep the meat frozen. This meant designing a machine to produce cold: a refrigerating machine. Harrison worked on this in between editing his newspaper and being elected to Parliament. In 1873 he was ready. The Americans had already developed a way of sending chilled meat by ship to England. Their method, keeping meat in a chamber surrounded by ice, worked for a short sea voyage. But the inside of the meat never became really cold and Harrison knew that deterioration would set in during the weeks it took to cross the oceans from Australia. His method froze the carcasses right through. In 1873 guests at a special banquet in Melbourne ate meat, poultry and fish that had been frozen and kept for six

85

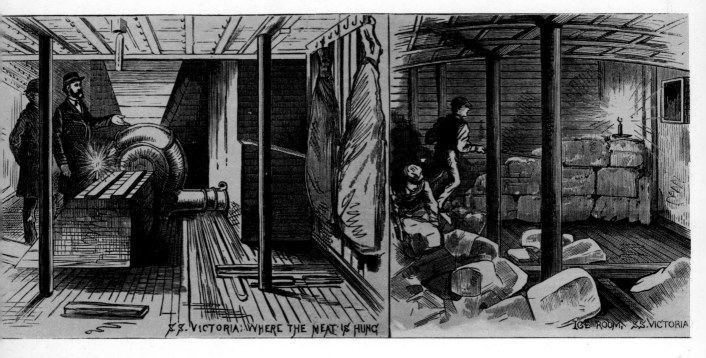

S.S. VICTORIA. WHERE THE MEAT IS HUNG

ICE ROOM, S.S. VICTORIA

Ice-cooled meat ship,
SS *Victoria*, 1877

months. "Equal to newly killed meat of good quality and full of flavour," said an enthusiastic guest. Later in the year, a ship fitted with Harrison's special refrigerated chamber sailed from Melbourne for London with twenty-five tons of frozen prime beef on board. But no one really knew how to handle the machinery, and the beef arrived partly thawed, and bad. Poor Harrison was ruined.

Several years later, in 1879, the first shipment of frozen food to reach its destination in an eatable condition arrived in France from the Argentine. Another Australian attempt, backed by business men and sheep owners, and using the method of a French inventor living in Sydney, had just failed. Two young Scottish shipowners finally solved the Australian problems with newly designed refrigerating equipment. Their first cargo of frozen meat and butter reached London on the steamer *Strathleven* early in 1880. Amidst great publicity and rejoicing, officials had a banquet on board and found the Australian food most enjoyable. A profitable trade began, carrying migrants to Australia and meat back.

Freezing can preserve food whole and raw. Now animal carcasses could be sent around the world. Refrigerated railway trucks shifted produce from where it was grown to where it was needed. Here, in addition to canning, which had been developed at the beginning of the century, was a new way of preserving surplus foods. Families began to install a new piece of kitchen equipment, the ice-box. And factories churned out tons of artificial ice.

Of the invention, the American author Mark Twain wrote:

In my time ice was jewelry; none but the rich could wear it. But anybody and everybody can have it now. I visited one of the ice factories in New Orleans, to see what the polar regions might look like when lugged into the tropics. But there was nothing striking in the aspect of the place. It was merely a spacious house, with some innocent steam machinery in one end of it and some big porcelain pipes running here and there. No, not porcelain — they merely seemed to be; they were iron, but the ammonia which was being breathed through them had coated them to the thickness of your hand with solid milk-white ice. It ought to have melted; for one did not require winter clothing in that atmosphere: but it did not melt; the inside of the pipe was too cold.

Sunk into the floor were numberless tin boxes, a foot square and two feet long, and open at the top end. They were full of clear water; and around each box salt and other proper stuff was packed; also, the ammonia gases were applied to the water in some way which will always remain a secret to me, because I was not able to understand the process. While the water in the boxes gradually froze, men gave it a stir or two with a stick occasionally — to liberate the air-bubbles, I think. Other men were continually lifting out boxes whose contents had become hard frozen. They gave the box a single dip into a vat of boiling water, to melt the block of ice free from its tin coffin, then they shot the block out upon a platform car, and it was ready for market. These big blocks were hard, solid, and crystal-clear. In certain of them, big bouquets of fresh and brilliant tropical flowers had been frozen in; in others, beautiful silken-clad French dolls, and other pretty objects. These blocks were to be set on end in a platter, in the centre of dinner-tables, to cool the tropical air; and also to be ornamental, for the flowers and things imprisoned in them could be seen as through plate glass. I was told that this factory could retail its ice, by wagon, through-out New Orleans, in the humblest dwelling-house quantities, at six or seven dollars a ton, and make a sufficient profit.

The trouble with frozen food was that it did not taste the same as fresh food. Some foods lost their flavour when they thawed, some became mushy and inedible. The reason was discovered by a German researcher, Max Planck, who was not directly interested in the food industry, but in the structure of crystals. Planck found that when fluids freeze, there is one temperature at which especially large crystals are formed; he called it the zone of maximum crystallization. The cells of foodstuffs are largely made up of fluid. Their zone of maximum crystallization is just below freezing point, between 25° and 31° F. The sharp edges of the large crystals tended to pierce the cell walls. Nothing showed as long as the food remained frozen. But as it thawed, the cell walls collapsed, the fluid ran out and the food became soggy and tasteless.

In the early 1920s Clarence Birdseye was in Labrador on a hunting trip. He noticed how fish, kept outside in the sub-zero temperature, froze immediately and tasted really good even months later. Of course, this is the way Eskimoes have always stored their food. Back in America, Birdseye experimented with ways of freezing fish as quickly as possible to preserve their flavour. Over several years he worked out methods of freezing food so fast that it went through the zone of maximum crystallization in a few minutes, instead of taking several hours as before. This

Clarence Birdseye

way, the large dangerous crystals had no time to form. No equipment existed for the quick freezing of food, so Birdseye had to develop his own machinery. By the end of the 1920s the first packages of frozen food were on the market.

Today, almost all foods can be bought frozen. A new era of ready-cooked foods has begun, changing our eating habits. But it took some years for Birdseye's methods to catch on. The public had to be persuaded that the old problems with frozen and chilled foods had been defeated. It was necessary to develop new marketing techniques. Frozen foods had to be kept at zero temperatures from start to finish, from processing plant to warehouse to delivery trucks to supermarkets to home storage.

*Dichloro-diphenyl-
trichloroethane*

In August 1944 the British government released the details to the press. "The full story can now be told of what has been described as one of the greatest scientific discoveries of the last decade, a synthetic multi-purpose insecticide which has already stopped a typhus epidemic, threatens the existence of the malaria-carrying mosquito and household insect pests, and is capable of controlling many of the insects which now do untold damage to food crops."

DDT, said an official, will be seen as the next most important contribution to the welfare of human beings to come out of the war, after penicillin.

DDT (dichloro-diphenyl-trichloroethane) was discovered by researchers in the laboratories of the Swiss firm of J. R. Geigy, in 1939, the year the Second World War began. The company's researchers had been looking for a better mothproofer for a long time. After they found one, they began looking for an insecticide which would act against a wider range of insects. When Dr Paul Müller synthesized dichloro-diphenyl-trichloroethane he had no idea that the resulting white crystals had such extraordinary insect-killing power. But the new compound could kill flies days after it had been sprayed on a window. Researchers tested its toxicity: what it was poisonous to, and how. In 1941 Gesarol, as the Swiss Company called it, stopped a plague of Colorado beetle which was threatening the Swiss potato crop. The chemists found that even a minute dose killed insects in two ways: if they came in contact with it, or if they ate it. Exposure to light did not weaken the effect of this synthetic insecticide, it did not dissolve in water and, best of all, it was very stable, very persistent. Areas treated by the new product would *go on* killing insects. Used as an insecticide, it was undoubtedly quite safe, researchers decided, then and later.

The Swiss were not in fact the first to discover dichloro-diphenyl-trichloroethane. A German student called Othmar Zeidler had prepared the compound back in 1874. He described it but had no idea that it was an insecticide.

In 1942 the Swiss firm managed to let its branches in the United States and Britain know about the new product. Both governments were immediately interested, and research and production became high wartime priorities. Someone at the British Ministry of Supply decided dichloro-diphenyl-trichloroethane was too long a name for the new compound and thought of DDT.

Officials decided that DDT should be used to combat health and hygiene problems, leaving its application to agriculture until after the war. This decision was made because wars had always killed more soldiers by disease than by wounds. More civilians died from wartime epidemics than from enemy action. DDT could kill the lice which carried typhus, one of the great plagues of war which spread among people living in crowded unclean conditions. It killed the flies which carried dysentery. And it killed the mosquito which carried the parasite which caused malaria. The typhus epidemic in the city of Naples in Italy during the winter of 1943-44 was brought under control in three weeks by a mass delousing of the population with dusting powder based on DDT. Troops going to Europe were issued with DDT-impregnated shirts, which kept their power of killing lice for two months even after washing. In the tropics, areas were sprayed with DDT to kill off mosquitoes and flies before troops went in.

DDT seemed a miracle discovery. The post-war possibilities were enormous, said the British government report in 1944. For example, each year in India, eighty million people suffered from malaria and two million of them died. DDT achieved remarkable results. Malaria was almost wiped out in many areas of the world. The populations of Ceylon, Madagascar, British Guiana, doubled as a result of anti-malaria campaigns using DDT. Those who survived malaria were left very weak; without the disease, people were healthier and therefore had greater resistance to other diseases. With this general improvement in health, more children lived, and so the problems of rocketing population and hunger suddenly became much worse in many parts of the world. At the same time, a new strain of malaria-carrying mosquitoes appeared, able to withstand the effect of DDT. The first house-flies immune to DDT were found in Italy as early as 1947. Lice resistant to DDT appeared during the Korean war. The hope of getting rid of all insect pests for ever did not last long. Insects turned out to be more adaptable and hardy than anyone had guessed.

DDT was the first of many powerful new synthetic insecticides which could kill the insects attacking crops. As a result, the food yield of farmers increased dramatically, helping to feed the world's hungry people. Insecticides are now essential to almost every part of food production all over the world. But it was found that DDT and other new

poisonous insecticides did after all have unwanted effects. In the beginning, DDT was praised because it lasted so long. Now it was discovered that it went on lasting — and that animals and humans were collecting DDT in their bodies. Some birds that ate insects killed by DDT died themselves. Fish were being killed by DDT-poisoned rivers and lakes. Seals in the Arctic and penguins in the Antarctic now have DDT in the fat of their bodies, because this substance spreads even to the world's wildernesses.

"Except for the antibiotics, it is doubtful that any material has been found which protects more people against more disease over a large area than does DDT," wrote scientists twenty years after DDT had been discovered. Many scientists still think that any risks DDT carries are outweighed by the protection it provides against the much worse dangers of malaria and typhoid in tropical countries, and by its contribution to increased food production. India has recently opened a new £4 million DDT manufacturing plant, and over half of the 180,000 tons of persistent pesticides produced in the world annually are used in tropical countries where alternative chemicals are so far either too specialized or too expensive. But, today, DDT is considered one of the pollutants that man has brought into the world and *must* take steps to control. Some countries have now placed a total ban on its use.

PENICILLIN

"This was the most dramatic experience to witness: the birth of a drug"

To understand the story of penicillin, we must forget that we know what penicillin can do. We must go back to a small crowded laboratory in a London hospital, in 1928. Dr Alexander Fleming was doing some research on bacteria. He was studying the staphylococcus bacteria, which cause many unpleasant and often dangerous infections. Examples of the bacteria were being grown by Fleming in small, glass culture dishes. Every now and then he would remove the lid from a dish and examine the bacteria under a microscope. One day Fleming came back from holiday and threw away some old culture dishes which had become spoilt by contamination. By chance an assistant came into his room, and Dr Fleming picked up several dishes to show him what a contaminated plate looked like. Then Fleming noticed a mould growing on the top edge of one of the dishes. It looked rather like the mould on cheese or bread.

When he was old and famous, Fleming always talked about the importance of chance in his life. "I have been wonderfully lucky, you know," he would tell students. Luck gave him a second look at something he had already thrown away. Fleming's trained eye noticed that the bacteria next to the patch of mould were shrivelling up, dissolving. "What had formerly been a well-developed staphylococcus colony was now but a shadow of its former self," he wrote.

What did this mean? Something made by the mould was destroying one of the powerful bacteria which attack man. Fleming decided to call this something penicillin, because it came from one of the penicillium moulds. That was the really big piece of luck. There are thousands of different moulds which could — and sometimes did — drift onto a culture dish and start growing. There are more than six hundred and fifty different penicillium moulds, but very few make penicillin. "That same mould might have dropped on many of my culture plates and there would have been no visible change to direct special attention to it. It might even have dropped on that same culture plate at a different stage of growth and shown nothing. However, somehow or other, everything fitted in and there was an appearance which called for investigation." All the same, Fleming said, "I had not the slightest suspicion that I was at the beginning of something extraordinary."

Very carefully Fleming drew a speck of the interesting

mould off the dish and put it in some nice warm broth where it could grow. After a few days he strained the broth to remove the mould, and began to investigate the liquid left behind — called mould juice by Fleming — which contained the mysterious penicillin. He found that it destroyed some bacteria, but did not affect others. He injected some of the mould juice into a healthy rabbit, then a mouse, to see if it was poisonous. It wasn't. Fleming's friends remember him asking if they had any old mouldy shoes lying around. If they had, he would take a little mould out of the damp, dark inside of the shoe and test it in the same way. He had to see if any other moulds had a similar effect on bacteria as his penicillin. They didn't.

Not many people took any notice of Alexander Fleming's discovery. Doctors and researchers had always been hoping to find something that would fight bacteria in the body — an antibiotic — without hurting the body itself, rather like a sort of magic bullet. Dr Fleming's penicillin did not seem harmful to the body cells. But Fleming was not able to find out what the mould juice really was, or how to keep it, or how to get the penicillin out of it. Nor were other researchers who tried in subsequent years. Mould juice by itself was no use to medicine.

Alexander Fleming might have stayed on at the small farm in Scotland where he was born and brought up, if his mother and brother had not decided to send him to London. He would probably have remained a clerk in a shipping office if he hadn't inherited a small legacy, and an elder brother suggested he use it to train to be a doctor.

Ten years after Fleming's discovery, a group of researchers at the University of Oxford decided to investigate thoroughly those naturally occurring substances that attack bacteria. In 1939 they began to study penicillin in detail, even though it was thought to be too unstable to spend much time on. No one was really thinking about possible medical benefits. It was a programme of research to find out answers to important problems. What was this penicillin? The head of the department, Dr Howard Florey (later Lord Florey), gathered together a team of specialists. Some of Fleming's original penicillin mould happened to be stored in a nearby laboratory.

Gradually the chemists in the team discovered ways to purify the mould juice and extract the penicillin from it. Penicillin was most unstable and difficult. "It vanishes almost while you look at it," they complained. The Oxford workers used new techniques which had been developed since Fleming tried, and developed more of their own. After eight months' hard work they had enough penicillin to make some crucial tests. They took healthy mice and infected them with bacteria. They injected some of the infected mice with penicillin and these lived, while the others not given penicillin died. The experiments proved that penicillin was truly less harmful to an animal's body than to the bacteria invading it. The crude powder used would prevent germs from multiplying even when diluted one in a million times. Later it was found that the powder used in these mouse experiments was so impure it contained less than 2 per cent of penicillin — yet it was successful. Old Dr Fleming read the results of the mice experiments and caught a train up to Oxford to see the precious penicillin. Dr Ernst Chain, one of the researchers, was amazed. He didn't know Fleming was still alive!

Penicillin must now be tried on human patients. Could it be a true antibiotic, something which would successfully fight harmful bacteria in the human body? A man is of course three thousand times the size of a mouse. Florey knew that much more penicillin would be needed. It was wartime. Britain was being bombed. The researchers rubbed spores of the mould on the insides of their pockets so that if a bomb fell, and one of the team escaped, the same strain of mould would be saved to be worked on elsewhere. Florey asked British chemical firms to help produce the necessary penicillin, but with the war raging no one could do it. The only thing left was to try to find ways of growing sufficient penicillin in the laboratory.

There weren't nearly enough containers. The mould was grown in biscuit tins, trays, pie-dishes, even in sixteen old-fashioned enamel bedpans. Laboratory assistants filled the containers with culture liquid and sowed it with spores of the mould. First a fine white hairy mould would appear on the surface of the culture liquid. Then it would turn bluish-green and become thick and wrinkled. After about a week the liquid under the mould would be yellow. Now the liquid had to be carefully removed and new fluid put in for the mould to feed off and grow more penicillin. It was a dreadfully tricky, uncomfortable, slow job. One germ could spoil the lot. But all this was simple compared to the actual extraction of penicillin from the crude mould juice. After purifying, each container of liquid would yield a tiny quantity of the fine brownish-yellow powder that was penicillin. The work went on for eight months before there was enough penicillin stored in the refrigerator to treat a human being.

In an Oxford hospital a policeman was dying of an acute infection. Nothing available could help him. The penicillin was tried and it worked, for five days. The policeman began to get better. "I remember very clearly still," one of the team said, "bicycling over to the laboratory in the evening, carrying the man's urine and the news of how he was doing. And Chain dancing with excitement at the possibility of a real triumph in medicine, and Florey reserved and quiet, but nonetheless intensely thrilled." Sadly, the precious powder ran out before the man was completely cured, the bacteria took over again in his body, and he died.

Howard Walter Florey came to England on a Rhod'es Scholarship to continue his study of medicine. He was born and brought up in Adelaide, South Australia.

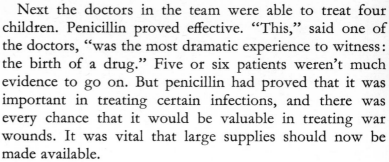

Next the doctors in the team were able to treat four children. Penicillin proved effective. "This," said one of the doctors, "was the most dramatic experience to witness: the birth of a drug." Five or six patients weren't much evidence to go on. But penicillin had proved that it was important in treating certain infections, and there was every chance that it would be valuable in treating war wounds. It was vital that large supplies should now be made available.

Howard Florey decided to go to the United States to try to persuade drug firms there to mass-produce penicillin. The laboratory methods worked out at Oxford were too slow and time-consuming, and the yield of penicillin from them was pitifully small. Ten to twenty gallons of mould juice was needed to treat a simple infection. Entirely new techniques had to be found, but this meant solving enormous new problems. Florey managed to persuade enough people in America to give the problems high priority. Several firms co-operated with researchers and the United States government, and the Oxford team handed over all the results of their work. Research and development did in fact cost millions and millions of dollars.

Yet even now, chance kept coming into the penicillin story. Researchers at Peoria, Illinois, had the job of getting the mould to produce more penicillin. They started hunting for a better strain of penicillin mould. All the penicillin so far made was descended from the original spore which landed on Alexander Fleming's work-bench back in 1928. Air-force men were asked to send samples of mould from all round the world to the laboratory at Peoria. None was any good. A laboratory assistant nicknamed Mouldy Mary had the job of going to the local market every day and bringing back all the mouldy fruit and vegetables she could find. One day she brought back a mouldy melon. Here was the energetic mould for which they had searched all over the world. Much of the penicillin used today is descended from that mouldy melon.

By 1943 penicillin was becoming available for wounded soldiers. "It was really on the invasion of Italy and Sicily when the drug went in almost with the bullet on the beaches that the most dramatic results were seen. Florey had the great excitement of waiting in North Africa and seeing the wounded men arrive with their wounds in a state never seen in history before. This meant not only the

saving of life, but saving of limbs, saving pain."

The public heard of penicillin. There was intense excitement. Here was a miracle drug. The yellow wonder powder! "I have never said that penicillin can cure *everything*," wrote Alexander Fleming. "It is the newspapers that have said that. It does have an extraordinary effect in certain cases of illness, but none in others. . . ." But people did not want to listen. They wanted to believe disease could now be defeated. Romantic, exaggerated stories were told about the discovery of penicillin. Fleming used to keep a cuttings book of all the untrue stories about him. Honours were heaped on the discoverers. Fleming and Florey were knighted. Fleming, Florey and Chain shared the Nobel Prize for Medicine in 1945.

Penicillin has saved hundreds of thousands of lives, and will go on doing so. We have probably all been treated with it, sometimes for quite minor things. Today it is one of many antibiotics available, and research goes on all the time for new ones. All the work at Oxford from 1939 to 1941 — the treatment of patients, the chemical, biological and bacteriological studies — was done with about four million units of hard-won penicillin. More than four million units can be given as a *single* dose these days. Penicillin is now truly everyday.

COCA-COLA

The mysterious "7X"

Old Dr Pemberton made patent medicines, such as *Globe Flower Cough Syrup*, *Gingerine* and *Extract of Styllinger* which people took hoping they would make them feel better. Then, one day in 1886, Dr Pemberton decided to try making a new drink, a tonic which would be especially good for hangovers, and for the nerves. He mixed essences, extracts and oils and took the mixture down to his friends at the local soda-fountain in Atlanta, Georgia. Soda-fountains had become popular in America as meeting-places where people could have a soft drink ("hard" meant alcohol) and something to eat such as an ice-cream. Soda-fountains had cool marble counter-tops and smart attendants to mix drinks. Soda-water had been invented by the famous English chemist, Dr Joseph Priestley, in 1772. But it was not made of soda — only distilled water charged with carbon dioxide gas, which bubbled and fizzed as it escaped. Ice-cream sodas were served at soda-fountains. They were invented in the city of Philadelphia in 1874, when an attendant dropped a dollop of ice-cream by mistake into a glass of soda, and someone discovered that it tasted good. Ice-cream sundaes were invented when ice-cream sodas were forbidden on Sundays in a town called Evanston, Illinois. A soda-fountain owner got around the law by serving ice-cream with syrup instead of soda.

Dr Pemberton tested the new drink, made some changes, and then tried them out. In the end he had a mixture everyone liked. All the flavours were so mixed up that the drink didn't taste of any particular one. It had its *own* taste. It wasn't too sweet. The soda-water made it bubbly, and it was an interesting dark-brown colour. One of Dr Pemberton's friends christened it Coca-Cola. John S. Pemberton decided to start manufacturing his invention. What Pemberton made was a syrup. A teaspoonful stirred into a glass of soda made the drink, Coca-Cola. The syrup itself was 99 per cent sugar and water. The other 1 per cent contained the essential ingredients — Coca-Cola's "secret recipe". Fourteen out of fifteen of these ingredients are pretty exactly known, because various law cases brought against the Coca-Cola Company have forced most of the facts into the open. The most famous was in 1909, brought by the United States government to investigate complaints that Coke was "harmful". The court overruled the case. As well as caramel, fruit flavours, various spices, phosphoric acid, coca leaves and cola nuts, Coca-Cola was found to contain caffeine, a stimulant. The fifteenth ingredient, the mysterious 7X, is one of the most closely guarded industrial secrets in the world. Not less than two and no more than three picked men ever know it at the same time, and they never travel together.

Asa Griggs Candler wanted to be a doctor but did not get far in his training; he became a pharmacist, working in an Atlanta store. He married his boss's daughter and was doing quite well when he drank his first Coca-Cola and decided it had possibilities. Old Pemberton's invention hadn't been very successful. The first year he sold only twenty-five gallons of Coca-Cola. Then he sold most of his shares in the invention for $283.29, and two years later he died. Candler bought up all the scattered shares easily because no one thought they were worth anything. Six years after Coke's invention, Candler, the farmer's son trained pharmacist turned business man, owned all the shares in Coca-Cola and set about really selling the drink.

Coca-Cola syrup began to be produced by the barrel-load at the factory in Atlanta. Candler decided that advertising was more important than anything else, and Coca-Cola signs began appearing on walls, in shops, magazines and soda-fountains, on awnings and glasses. In 1899 two men who liked going to baseball matches decided it was a great pity they couldn't have their favourite

drink right at the game, instead of waiting to get to a soda-fountain where an attendant had to mix it. They travelled to Atlanta and asked Mr Candler if they could have the right to put Coca-Cola in bottles and sell it. Candler agreed and went on making Coca-Cola syrup while others worked at bottling and distribution. It was wonderfully easy stuff to make. And it was extremely profitable. The two baseball-loving bottlers made fortunes, and soon Candler himself was a multi-millionaire. All kinds of imitations and alternative soft drinks were put on the market, over a thousand of them, but none succeeded like Coke, in its famous bottle. In 1919 Candler sold his company for twenty-five million dollars. The new owners went on expanding sales and making more millions of dollars.

Coca-Cola is phenomenally successful. It is the most popular soft drink in the world. And it is the most widely advertised product in the world. After all, the recipe is still the same, the method of making the drink hasn't really changed for seventy-five years, so the only way of selling more Cokes is by persuading more people to drink them. The advertising always emphasizes that Coke is a wholesome, clean-living drink, for every member of the family. When America joined in the Second World War the head of the company declared that no GI anywhere should ever go thirsty for a Coke. One of the first jobs after the United States armed forces established beachheads in North Africa and France was the construction of Coca-Cola bottling plants.

Coca-Cola is always thought of as an especially American drink. Yet in 1964 seventy-five million Cokes a day were downed in 127 different countries. By early 1974 the total had reached over 165 million, in more than 135 countries of the world.

Gobble, gulp and go

John Harvey Kellogg, his brother Will Keith and all their fourteen other brothers and sisters ate hot pancakes with bacon fat and molasses most days for breakfast. Mrs Kellogg got up early, stoked the fire, and had the pancakes cooking before anyone came down to eat. The Kelloggs lived in a log cabin in the Michigan forest, then in a small house in the small town of Battle Creek, Michigan. Life was tough and not much fun. The children were expected to earn their living in their father's broom factory as soon as they were able.

Mr and Mrs Kellogg belonged to a strict religious group called the Seventh Day Adventists, who believed that the Sabbath was on a Saturday. They also believed in health reform, which meant using water as a cure for illnesses, and eating a simple diet with no tea, coffee, alcohol, tobacco, spices, and also, they eventually decided, no meat. Battle Creek was the Adventist headquarters; here the group set up a medical boarding-house where people could be treated for their illnesses by following Adventist teaching on diet and behaviour. But the Health Reform Institute was still very small when, in 1876, John Harvey Kellogg, now a young doctor, took over. He ran it for the next sixty-five years.

Dr John had plenty of ideas about diet. As a medical student in New York he had a barrel of apples and a barrel of a special biscuit called Graham Crackers in his room. Every morning he ate seven Graham Crackers and two apples, helped out by one coconut a week and occasionally potatoes and oatmeal. With this diet he put on seventeen pounds and felt fit.

The Battle Creek Sanitarium became very popular, even world-famous. ("The word is *Sanatorium,*" it was pointed out. "I don't care," replied Dr John, who had probably made a spelling mistake. "Sanatorium means a rest home for wounded soldiers; Sanitarium will mean something different.") Overweight ladies and their overworried business-men husbands came to rest, exercise, diet and breathe fresh air. Dr John was a marvellous host, and there was plenty of occupation: games, lectures, concerts. The very ill came to 'The San' as well, and, when possible, poor people who could not afford to pay were given free attention. John Kellogg worked extraordinarily hard. He didn't believe in holidays, so neither could his staff. He wrote over eighty books, and hundreds of articles

John Harvey Kellogg

101

about his various medical and dietary beliefs. He travelled overseas, developed a new type of stitching for surgical use, and at the peak of the Sanitarium's popularity was looking after twelve hundred guests at a time.

People a hundred years ago ate very badly by today's standards. Since the beginning of time, man's problem has been to get *enough* to eat — and it still is for much of the world's population. In the United States there was plenty of food, but people always seemed to bolt it down in a hurry — gobble, gulp and go. Out west, the diet was far too monotonous: coffee, hog and hominy (a maize porridge) for every meal. In big cities the rich overate. It would take twelve hours' hard physical labour to use up the energy produced by a meal which included two or three kinds of meat, fish and game, plus spices and pickles. But more and more people were now living sedentary lives; their stomachs just could not cope with such huge meals.

A stay at the Battle Creek Sanitarium made patients think about the importance of a good diet, probably for the first time in their lives. Dr John Kellogg believed in a proper diet, not drugs, to cure illness. Meat, alcohol and smoking were strictly forbidden at Battle Creek Sanitarium, because of Adventist teaching. But the vegetarian meals served in the dining-room were very monotonous, and some patients left because they did not like the food. Others would sneak off to the Red Onion, a café in town where they could get steak and chops.

From the beginning Dr John Kellogg experimented in the kitchens with new, appetizing ways of preparing vegetarian foods. He invented Granola, which looked like

Battle Creek Sanitarium
c. 1890

toasted breadcrumbs, and he also invented peanut butter. The cooking of cereals converted some of the starch in the grains to dextrin and so made them easier to digest. He used the things vegetarians are allowed to eat, such as nuts, grain and vegetables, to invent foods that tasted like the things they were not allowed to eat. Protose was like beef, Nuttose like veal, and Caramel Cereal tasted like coffee. Ex-patients began to ask for supplies of the Sanitarium health foods, so Dr Kellogg set up small companies to manufacture his inventions, and sent his foods to his customers by mail order.

In the middle of Dr John's experimenting, an inventor called Henry D. Perky made a machine for shredding wheat, and sold the resulting little pillow-shaped product as Shredded Wheat. People liked it. Then a business man called Charles W. Post came to the Sanitarium for a cure, but spent most of his time in the kitchens and laboratories. He thought that Dr John Kellogg's cereal substitute for coffee was a magnificent idea for making money, and offered to go into business with Kellogg, who angrily refused. The good name of the Sanitarium should not be involved in selling something commercially, and certainly not in advertising. But Post knew that because of the San, the name Battle Creek meant healthy living and good diet to Americans. So he set up a factory in Battle Creek, and started to manufacture his own cereal substitute for coffee, called Postum. Post advertised heavily and cleverly. "Do you suffer from coffee headaches? Take Postum." "POSTUM MAKES RED BLOOD." Soon he invented Grape-Nuts, a hard, chewy cereal food. Grape-Nuts was advertised as being beneficial for the appendix, malaria, loose teeth, and the brain. Post's profits went up so fast he was a multi-millionaire within seven years.

Will Keith Kellogg was Dr John's younger brother. He worked at the Sanitarium doing all the organizing, and tidying up jobs left unfinished by his energetic famous brother. Probably Will Keith's efficient administration kept the Sanitarium going — certainly everyone brought their problems to him to solve. What part did Will Keith play in the invention of the various food products? It is difficult to know, because the two brothers did not get on very well. Dr John pushed Will Keith around, treating him almost like a servant. He would ride around the Sanitarium grounds on a bicycle, to keep fit, while Will

Will Keith Kellogg was the seventh son of a seventh son, born on the seventh day of the seventh month, all of which he considered to be very significant.

103

had to trot alongside taking down notes and instructions. Later they fought each other in the law courts over everything they could think of, and the feud never ended. "The Kellogg women can be loving," said one of their sisters, "but the Kellogg men can be *mean*."

Dr John and Will Keith Kellogg made the first precooked flaked cereal in 1894. They were looking for a digestible substitute for bread and had no idea they were inventing a breakfast food — the phrase did not even exist. Dr John was experimenting with wheat, which he boiled for varying lengths of time, and then pushed through rollers. Will scraped the sticky dough off the rollers with a knife. Nothing useful could be done with this mess. One batch of boiled wheat got left for several days; no one had time to do anything with it. In the end the brothers decided to put it through the rollers, although it was very mouldy, to see what would happen. Out came large thin flakes, each grain of wheat forming one flake. The flakes were baked in the oven and emerged crisp and tasty. After more experimenting, the Kelloggs found out how to leave the boiled wheat long enough to produce flakes, without the wheat becoming mouldy.

Even though they were tough and rather tasteless, the wheat flakes were instantly popular with the Sanitarium patients. The secret of how to make them leaked out; soon there were dozens of manufacturers copying the recipe.

Battle Creek suffered a breakfast-food rush. Post's success, and the various Kellogg inventions, brought hundreds of hopeful money-makers into the town to try their luck at making a breakfast food in a box. There were dozens of recipes, using wheat, corn, rice, oats—roasting and boiling them, squeezing, rolling or cutting them up. One sack of wheat from the farmer could be transformed into hundreds of cartons filled with flakes and puffs, and a large profit—or so everyone hoped. Temporary factories sprang up. Investors talked busily on street corners. But the craze didn't last long, and most of the companies failed. The makers of Cero-Fruito, Tryabita, Tryachewa, Nutrita, My Food, Per-fo, Malt-Ho and Maple-Flakes gave up their dreams of instant fortunes from breakfast foods.

Will Keith Kellogg could see all the Sanitarium food inventions being taken over and developed by other people. He was determined not to let this happen to the best invention of them all, corn flakes. A method for making

corn flakes had been worked out about four years after
the wheat flakes. At the age of forty-six, when he already
thought himself an old man, Will Keith Kellogg began a
new career. He left the Sanitorium, collected together
money to start a factory, paid Dr John a large amount for
his share in the corn-flake invention, and set up in Battle
Creek the Toasted Corn Flake Company. All his savings
went into the scheme. The Doctor heartily disapproved.
Quarrelling soon broke out between the brothers and law
cases started over who had the right to do what: who could
use the name Kellogg, for example, in the manufacture of
breakfast foods. Dr John had always refused to use the
family name on any of the Sanitarium products. Now,
when Will Keith began to use it, he decided he would too.
After all, who was *the* famous Kellogg? When Will Keith
Kellogg wrote out his first cheque for a million dollars he
said he had never wanted or expected to be rich, but other
people had made him rich by trying to push him around.
He just dug in his toes and became determined to win.

The packets of corn flakes rolled out of Will Keith's factory in Battle Creek in ever increasing numbers. The taste of corn flakes had been improved by adding malt, sugar and salt for flavour. Will Keith argued that since there were more well people than sick people, corn flakes must be advertised as good to eat, and not treated just as a health food. To fight off imitators, every packet had this message, in red ink: *The original bears this signature—W. K. Kellogg.* Will Keith was determined people should not get muddled over who was producing corn flakes. Like Post, with Postum, he spent huge amounts on advertising, using especially the new invention, radio. Free samples of Toasted Corn Flakes were given away to millions of housewives. Breakfast-food manufacturers were some of the first to concentrate on *children:* if children wanted Kellogg's Corn Flakes, then their mothers would probably buy them. Give-away presents were included in each packet: cut-outs, sets of cards, models. Kellogg's developed other cereal products: for example, All Bran and Rice Krispies. W.K. became known as the "Cornflake King", and his products were made and sold around the world. Fifty years after the company began, the factories at Battle Creek alone produced six million packets of cereals a day, and a million of these were corn flakes.

When he was seventy years old, Will Keith Kellogg started a third career: giving away his money. A foundation was set up with most of the Kellogg Corn Flake fortune. Its especial interest was, and still is, helping needy children. The foundation also gives money to hospitals, schools and research centres. To the end of his life Will Keith hated all publicity. He was a rather difficult, shy, simple old man, very different from his popular, bossy, enthusiastic brother. Dr John Kellogg and his wife had no children of their own, but one way or another they collected forty-two boys and girls and brought them up in their home. Will Keith Kellogg argued so often with his son that the young man left the company, and the old man found he had no member of his family to carry on the business.

Will Keith Kellogg did not achieve his final ambition: to live longer than Dr John. Both brothers died when they were ninety-one, but the imperious old Dr John managed three more months of his ninety-second year than Will Keith.

THE SEWING-MACHINE

Only one of the sewing-machine's early inventors was a tailor. At the beginning of the nineteenth century Barthelemy Thimmonier was quite happy to invent himself out of a job, but a furious French crowd did not agree. They destroyed his eighty sewing-machines, which were busy making uniforms for the French army, and nearly killed Thimmonier himself. His neighbours were certain he was a little mad: spending four years trying to make a *machine* sew! Until the sewing-machine was invented, every stitch in every piece of cloth had to be made by hand. Tailors had complained of bent backs and sore eyes for centuries. Girls had to learn needlework if they wanted to be good wives. Working at top speed, a tailor could sew thirty stitches a minute. Even Thimmonier's inefficient sewing-machine could make two hundred stitches a minute. But he died poor and broken-hearted, his machines hated and destroyed.

The same fate nearly happened to Elias Howe. Howe was born twenty-six years after Thimmonier, in America, and was just as determined to make a machine do the work of sewing. He was working in a machine shop in Boston when he heard his employer say to an inventor: "Why

"I don't care a damn for the invention. The dimes are what I'm after"

TAILOR

waste time on a knitting-machine? Why don't you try to invent a sewing-machine? *That* will make you a fortune." The twenty-year-old Howe thought, "Why don't *I*?"

Howe worked steadily at the machine. He was finally reduced to boarding at the house of a friend who agreed to support his family and the inventing process in return for a half share in this far-fetched sewing-machine. Howe was frail and often sick, and so poor that his wife took in sewing to earn a little money for the family. He used to watch her sewing for hours, then try to make a machine that copied all the actions of the human hand. It failed because the movements were far too complicated. Howe only began to succeed when he stopped thinking about the process of hand-sewing and started trying to achieve the same result by different methods. Many inventors have nearly gone mad trying to invent machines that imitate the human body.

After several years' work Howe patented a machine in 1846. He made two suits on it, one for his friend and one for himself, to show how strong the stitching was. The machine could only sew in straight lines a short distance at a time before the cloth had to be moved for a fresh start. Another problem was that the thread kept breaking. But the machine did make a lock stitch which would not undo when it was pulled. As the thread passed through the material and began to make a loop, a bobbin underneath pushed another thread through the loop and pulled it tight. The secret here was to have the eye in the *point* of the needle and not the head, reversing the sewing process completely; all needles since the first cave men stitched skins together with a bone needle and sinew had the eye at the other end. Howe took a long time to stumble on this solution, though in fact it had already been discovered about twelve years earlier by Walter Hunt, the remarkable New York inventor. Hunt, so the story goes, asked his daughter if he should patent the sewing-machine he had invented. No, she said, it will be "injurious to the interests of hand-sewers"—the familiar old reason.

No one was interested in buying Elias Howe's machine, even though he raced it successfully against hand-sewers, and crowds always gathered to watch it work. It was very expensive and not very efficient. In despair, Howe asked his brother to try to sell it in England. A manufacturer of corsets, umbrellas and leather bags, all of them stitched by

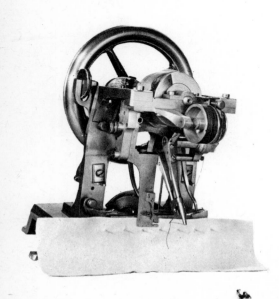

Elias Howe's sewing-machine, 1845

hand, immediately bought the machine and the right to sell it in England for £250. Howe was offered a job at £3 a week, adapting his sewing-machine for the heavier task of sewing leather. The Howe family sailed for England in 1847. Elias quarrelled with his employer and left. Now he was even poorer than before. He borrowed enough money to send his wife and children back to America, then worked his way home cooking for passengers on an emigrant ship. When he arrived in New York he heard that his wife was dying—and his household goods had been lost at sea.

In the middle of all his misery Howe noticed that while he had been away the sewing-machine had begun to interest people. There were other models like his machine. Howe gathered all his energies, borrowed money, and decided to contest the patents of the companies manufacturing sewing-machines, in particular Isaac Singer's. The newspapers called it the "sewing-machine war". In the end, the judges decided that Elias Howe had invented the basic sewing-machine and each manufacturer had to pay him a royalty—a small fee—for every sewing-machine they made. In fact, it became impossible for anyone to make a sewing-machine without infringing on someone else's patent, so the major companies got together, gave up their battles in the law courts, pooled all their patents, and got on with the business of making and selling. Howe became a very rich man very quickly. But his wife had died before all the years of poverty and struggle paid off, and Howe himself died when he was only forty-eight.

The sewing-machine was the first important labour-saving device in the home. The man who got it there was Isaac Singer. Singer made the sewing-machine into big business. "I don't care a damn for the invention," he said. "The dimes are what I'm after."

Isaac Singer was another poor boy, almost illiterate, the eighth child of a German immigrant to America. He ran away from home when he was twelve and became an actor, working as a machinist whenever he had to. Like Howe, Singer was in a Boston machine shop when someone suggested he could make his fortune out of a really practical sewing-machine. (He had already patented two inventions, a machine for drilling rock and a wood-carving machine.) But Singer was now nearly forty, and had one official wife with two children, and another unofficial wife with six children, and he needed money. It was 1850 and at

STRIVE TO EXCEL.

W. S. & C. H. THOMSON'S SKIRT MANUFACTORY.

PATENT INDESTRUCTABLE

Wood engraving from
Harper's Weekly, 1859

least ten sewing-machines had appeared, which more or less copied Elias Howe's machine, and, like Howe's, were not very efficient. In fact, Singer invented the first sewing-machine which really worked well, thinking up in about two weeks several brilliant improvements to the design of existing machines.

The next problem was how to sell a machine which cost $110 when the average American family earned only $500 a year? A sewing-machine was a luxury. Isaac Singer was a noisy showman and an actor salesman. "Come and see a machine sew a pair of trousers in forty minutes!" Pretty girls sewed on Singer machines in shop windows while the crowds gathered. World-wide advertising and persistent salesmen knocking on doors put Singer sewing-machines into homes in every country on the globe. Advanced business techniques, mostly thought up by Singer's partner, a sober lawyer, made sure that mechanics were available everywhere to repair and service machines. The prejudice that women were too stupid to handle a machine had to be overcome. I. M. Singer & Co. offered their product at half price to community leaders such as clergymen and teachers. Sewing-machines could be bought on instalment and this was considered a very daring and dangerous innovation.

Isaac Singer blossomed with his new wealth. The manufacturing costs of his machine were as low as $23. He lived in great style in New York. He thought up, and patented, a jumbo carriage painted vivid yellow drawn by nine horses, seating thirty-one passengers, with a nursery at the back "with beds to put the dear ones to sleep". (Now there were eighteen Singer children, one way or another.) A small orchestra could be accommodated on the outside, along with guards to keep off intruders. "A regular steam-boat on wheels . . . a monster," said a New York news-paper. Singer's partner was greatly embarrassed by these extravagances, and by the immorality of Singer's private life, just when the firm was trying to sell the sewing-machine to respectable families. The scandals became too much and Singer went to France, where he found a charm-ing half-English girl who married him. After a few years he retired from the business and took his wife and their six children to a great estate near Torquay on the English coast. He built a palace with colonnades and marble halls and a completely equipped theatre, for half a million dollars; he nicknamed it The Wigwam. His neighbours thought him odd, but agreed that he was friendly and very generous. Here he happily entertained any of his twenty-four children who happened to visit. When he died, they all squabbled over the will.

The sewing-machine was quickly adapted to anything which needed stitching: especially shoes and leather work, also book-binding and carpets. It revolutionized clothing, giving birth to the vast ready-made clothing industry. Before the advent of the sewing-machine, tailors used to put any extra suits they made on sale as "ready-made" clothes. These were especially popular in ports, for home-coming sailors. Now clothes were made in factories with newly invented cutting and pressing machines, and power-ful sewing-machines stitching yards of seam a minute. War, especially the American Civil War which began in 1861, gave a tremendous boost to the new industry. Tens of thousands of new uniforms were needed, fast. The govern-ment collected the soldiers' measurements, and for the first time average sizes were worked out, which greatly helped in mass-producing clothes. Manufacturers realized that a man with a certain size chest usually had arm, leg and waist measurements in proportion.

The invention of the sewing-machine did help the housewife at home. At last one of her many jobs, sewing the family's clothes by hand, could be done by machine. But her real freedom came when she could go to a shop and buy everything the family wore *ready-made*. Yet, at the same time as factories turned out more and more ready-made clothing, clothes were also produced in what are now called "sweated labour" conditions. Towards the end of the last century, especially in overcrowded cities like New York, there were thousands of poor immigrants willing to work for low wages, just to get employment. Families bought or hired a sewing-machine and everyone, even the children, worked at home in dark, dirty conditions, sewing together pieces of clothing handed out by the manufacturers. Many immigrants from Europe began and ended their lives in America working in these conditions as slaves of a machine which had been meant to lighten the sewers' labour. People wanted many more clothes now that they could be obtained ready-made, and fashions kept changing, and so the demand for sewing-machines was great.

Edison invented a sewing-machine with a motor which was run by the sound of the human voice. A membrane mounted just level with the sewer's mouth transformed the sound of the voice into power. Edison told the lady to recite poetry into it, or read aloud. Unfortunately, it turned out to be just as tiring to talk all the time as treadle, and the modulations of the human voice caused the machine to work irregularly.

Did Ellen suggest the idea to Ebenezer, or did Ebenezer ask Ellen to help him work out the new notion? Whoever thought of it first, Mr and Mrs Ebenezer Butterick's brainchild was an instant success.

Ebenezer was just an ordinary tailor making shirts in a small town in Massachusetts, U.S.A. The idea was to design a pattern out of paper so that *anyone* could make a shirt, as often as they liked. The Buttericks experimented for four years until the first patterns, cut from stiff paper and hand-folded by the family, were ready to sell on 16th June 1863. They were so cheap and so useful that they were immediately successful.

Mr and Mrs Ebenezer Butterick's brainchild

Butterick patterns 1867:
Nos 60 and 155 are for
Garibaldi jackets.

Garibaldi in 1865

113

Ellen and Ebenezer moved later that year to a bigger town where they could sell the patterns more easily. Ellen felt that mothers all over the country would be delighted if they could buy patterns to make their children's clothes at home, especially on one of the newly invented sewing-machines. She was right. The Garibaldi suit was a sensational success. Giuseppe Garibaldi had just finished fighting to unify Italy into one nation. He was an international hero. The Buttericks' first paper pattern for children's clothes was modelled on the colourful uniform worn by the hero and his men. Soon there were little Garibaldis all over America.

Women, so the Buttericks were told, were begging for patterns to make themselves clothes too. Ellen and Ebenezer obliged, and business expanded so fast that they moved the pattern-making factory from their home to a disused school, then to a factory in New York. Patterns in graded sizes were now cut out of tough, thin tissue paper, and a magazine published by the Buttericks reported on the latest fashions. Eight years after the first paper pattern appeared, the company sold six million. Five years after that they had branches in London, Paris, Berlin and Vienna.

No one thought of anything even a little bit like the zipper until Whitcomb L. Judson came along. There were buttons and button-holes, hooks and eyes, laces, buckles. They all took an irritatingly long time to do up, especially when men wore high-laced boots and fashionable ladies squeezed themselves into long corsets.

Whitcomb L. Judson's slide-fastener was an out-of-the-blue invention, and no one knows what gave him the idea. No one even knows much about him, except that he was a mechanical engineer living in Chicago and that he patented other inventions, to do with a street railway system and motor-cars.

Judson invented the first zipper (called, at the time, a Clasp Locker or Unlocker) in 1891. This ingenious little device looks so simple, and the principle behind it is simple: one row of hooks and eyes slotting neatly into another row by means of a tab. Yet it took twenty-two years, many improvements and another inventor to make the zipper really practical.

The zipper had to be produced cheaply, because no one would pay a lot of money for it. So Judson invented a

They called the galoshes "Zippers"

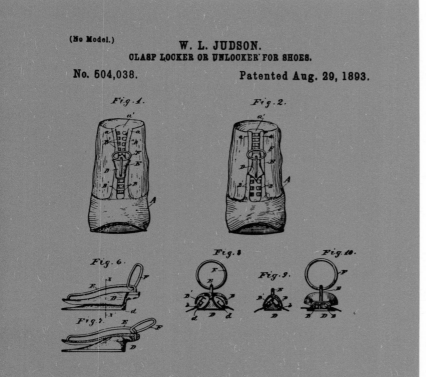

W. L. Judson's patent 1893

machine to mass-produce his slide-fastener. But the machine was terribly complicated and kept on breaking down. In 1905 Judson invented a new fastener, the C-curity, which was easier to manufacture. Clothing manufacturers, however, were not the least bit interested in trying out the fasteners, so the only way Judson could get them onto the market was by letting pedlars sell them from door to door as novelties. Moreover, the C-curity was stiff and clumsy, and had a bad habit of bursting open at inconvenient times.

Gideon Sundback, a young Swedish engineer, came to work for Judson's struggling company. He thought hard and decided that the interlocking parts needed to be much smaller to give the fastener greater flexibility and to stop it bursting open. After several attempts, Sundback invented in 1913 a really practical fastener which is in all important ways the same as the one we use today. He also invented the necessary machinery to manufacture it cheaply.

Clothing manufacturers still refused to use the fastener. But in 1918 an inventor showed the American army a flying suit he had invented which happened to use the slide-fastener. The army put the suit through such tough tests it disintegrated—all except the fastener! A Navy officer happened to see the tests, and Judson's unknown little company got an order for ten thousand fasteners. Next, Judson's invention was used in the manufacture of gloves and tobacco pouches. Then B. F. Goodrich & Company put the fasteners into their rubber galoshes. They called the galoshes "Zippers"—which is how the slide-fastener got its popular name.

The fifty-second man to attempt the invention of a successful writing machine was Christopher Latham Sholes. Frenchmen, Austrians, Italians, Swiss, Englishmen, Russians, Americans had been trying for at least a hundred and fifty years before Sholes started. Some of the machines made raised letters for blind people to read with their fingertips. Some had letters which were arranged like keys on a piano and were almost as large—and so really rather clumsy. All the machines had one great problem. They were as slow or slower than writing with a pen. The first inventor of a writing machine, an English engineer called Henry Mill, had the right idea. He described it as "An Artificial Machine or Method for the Impressing or Transcribing of Letters Singly or Progressively one after another, as in Writing, whereby all Writings whatsoever may be Engrossed in Paper or Parchment so Neat and Exact as not to be distinguished from Print". Queen Anne granted him a patent in 1714, but not even a drawing survives of his invention.

The first writing machine in America had been invented in the backwoods up near the Great Lakes by a surveyor called William Austin Burt, in 1829. Burt's Typographer was a clever machine. The letters were arranged on a semicircular band of metal which moved to bring each letter to the printing point as it was needed, rather like a hand-held labelling machine today. The editor of the local newspaper saw the real possibilities of the machine. "This is a specimen of the printing done by me on Mr. Burt's Typographer," he wrote to the President of the United States. "You will observe some inaccuracies in the situation of the letters; these are owing to the imperfections of the machine, it having been made in the woods of Michigan where no proper tools could be obtained by the inventor. . . . I am satisfied . . . that the Typographer will be ranked with the most novel, useful and pleasing inventions of this age." This promoter did not have any money to back the Typographer, so he took Burt down to the big city, New York, to find someone who would invest money in developing and manufacturing it. No one was interested. Burt didn't mind. He went back to his log cabin and finished inventing something he considered much more important: a surveying compass that used the sun to find direction instead of the earth's magnetic attraction. It became United States government standard equipment for the next seventy-five years.

"It piles an awful stack of words on one page"

First letter written on
Burt Typographer, 1830

New-York March, 13, 1830

Dear Companion,

I have but jest got my second machine into operation and this is the first specimen I send you except a few lines I printed to regulate the machine, I am in good health but am in fear these lines will not find youse and the children from the malencholley account your letter gave m of sickness and ths in our neighbourhod, I had rested contented to what I should if it had been summer season about the health of my family, as it is jenerly healthy during the winter months; but

heir has ben an unusual quentity of sickness hoars this winter, and it has ben very cold in Urope as well as in America, a strong indication of the change of weemonth, that I have so often mentioned.— Mr Sheldon arrive hre four days ago he went imediately on to Washington and took my modile for the Pattent Office, he will return hre next week at which time I shall put my machine on sale and shall ceil out the patent as soon a I cold return home, at anoy rate I seall roturne home as soon a the Lake navigation is open if life and health is spared me. I have got along but sb since I have been hre for the want of cash to hire such elp as I wanted; I have be as prudent as I could, have taken my board with a family from Xyuga who keep a bording house they are very good christian people and re kind to me. I pay three Dolars a week for my board.—You must excuse mistakes, the above is printed among a croud of people asking me many questions about the machine. Tell th boys that I have some present for them. If I had ney news to communicate I would print more but as I have no I must close hoping these lines will find you well I wish you to write as soon you receive this, do not make any excuse I shall like si it in any shape

William A. Burt.

Phobe Burt

Christopher Latham Sholes, a gentle, tall, thin man who was a moderately successful newspaper man, printer, and local politician, liked spending his spare time in a Milwaukee, Wisconsin, machine shop with his friends, designing things. Carlos Glidden was making a spading machine which he thought should replace the plough, and would bring him a fortune. Sam Soulé was helping Sholes invent a large heavy piece of machinery for numbering pages. If you can do that, said Glidden, why can't you make a machine that will print words as well as figures? Sholes didn't take much notice, but a few months later he read an article in a magazine describing several inventors' attempts to design a mechanical writer. Why don't I try, thought Sholes. There were plenty of good reasons why people continued their efforts to invent a writing machine. The fastest anyone could write with a pen was thirty words a minute, and that was really annoyingly slow, besides being difficult to read. In 1844 Samuel Morse demonstrated his electric telegraph to the United States government. Now telegraphers could send and receive a message in code much faster than they could write it down. And shorthand secretaries could take notes as quickly as a man could speak—yet they had to be written out slowly by hand. A personal printing-press would speed things up wonderfully.

The middle of the last century was a time in America when people believed that with the right tools and materials, and with some luck, you could invent almost anything to do whatever you wanted. Many Americans did a little inventing on the side. Even Abraham Lincoln, sixteenth President of the United States, came to the White House with several inventions patented: a new method of steering a wagon, for example, and special balloons to lift boats off river shoals. Inventors could usually find someone to back their brainchildren with money, and promote them, because if they worked—that was the way to get rich fast. There were several thousand inventions patented in the United States every year that got nowhere. Plenty of backers lost all their money. But Americans really believed everyone should try to be a millionaire. If you lost one way, you might make it another. All the failed ideas, the wasted money, the wrong inventions at the wrong time, are not remembered. The success stories are famous just because the inventions were successful.

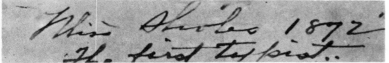

Miss Sholes typing at her
father's machine, 1872

Sholes thought about the problem of how to arrange the letters on a writing machine. It should be possible to put them around the edge of a wheel, like his numbering machine. One night when he could not sleep, a better idea came. Each letter, or "type", could be put on a separate bar so that each could strike the paper and make a letter independently from the others. In fact, unknown to Sholes, this method had been worked out by a Frenchman over thirty years before. During the next couple of days Sholes got a sheet of the newly invented carbon paper from the town telegraph office and rigged up a little machine using odds and ends, which tried out his principle with one letter, W. WWWWWWW it typed. With help from his friends Glidden and Soulé, and one of the mechanics from the machine shop, Sholes built a complete writing machine. He was now forty-eight years old. "C. LATHAM SHOLES, SEPT. 1867" he typed on it. They built an improved model and Sholes wrote—using the new machine

—to everyone he could think of, asking for financial backing. He wrote to a big, loud, red-faced man, James Densmore, with whom he had once published a newspaper. "I'll come immediately," Densmore replied. He liked the idea of a writing machine as much as William Austin Burt's newspaper editor had forty years earlier.

Densmore agreed to pay the back bills: $600, plus expenses to come, in return for a share in the profits of the machine. In fact, although Densmore had invented and patented the first oil tank for a railway truck, he had very little money. When Densmore got to Milwaukee he was shocked to see how clumsy and crude the writing machine was. He demanded improvements: it must be lighter and simpler. This went on for six years. Sholes, at first with help from the others, made over thirty different models of his Type-Writer, each improving on the last. The experimental machines were sent to shorthand reporters for them to try out. They would work well, clattering along much faster than a pen, and then something would go wrong. The type bars bunched and stuck; the string holding the weight would break. Back the machines came, with all the faults listed, and Sholes had to get down to redesigning the mechanism. Two years after he began, he wrote to a friend: "I think the machine is now as perfect in its mechanism as I know how to make it, or to have it made. . . ."

Wheatstone typewriter, 1851

Poor Sholes. Every time he thought he had finished, Densmore kept him at it, criticizing, enthusiastic, pushing. "If it is worth anything, it is worth a vast amount," Densmore declared. He never gave up believing in the Type-Writer, even when other enthusiasts dropped out and Sholes was ready to stop. "In general, the invention and the success of it have been all right from the beginning," Densmore wrote to his brother, "but there have been constant minor, subordinate difficulties that have proved quite formidable; and these minor difficulties have caused us a great deal of delay and a vast amount of expense." At times Sholes worked sixteen hours a day on the latest improved model, and the money to pay for it was always spent before it arrived.

Sholes's Type-Writer combined most of the ideas already discovered by previous inventors. It could type only in capitals, and was assembled in such a way that you could not see what you had typed until you had finished. But it was fast. The rather odd order of letters on the keyboard of our typewriters today — QWERTYUIOP —was worked out by Sholes. He put the most commonly used letters farthest away from each other to stop the type bars from colliding. More efficient arrangements have been worked out since, but no one will change the layout of the keys. It would mean unlearning the familiar keyboard.

At last Densmore decided the machine was good enough to sell. He tried manufacturing it himself, unsuccessfully. Then in 1873 he took it to Remingtons, manufacturers of guns, sewing-machines and farm machinery. The American Civil War had ended by now, so fewer guns were being made and Remingtons had some factory space. Two of their top mechanics adapted the Type-Writer for mass-production. Because they were sewing-machine men, the Remington Model 1, the first commercially available typewriter, looked rather like a sewing-machine. It was a curiously shaped, shiny black metal box with flowers stencilled on its front and sides, perched on a stand with a foot-treadle carriage return.

I AM TRYING TTO GET THE HANG OF THIS NEW FFANGLED WRITING MACHINE, BUT AM NOT MAKING A SHINING SUCCESS OF IT.... THE MACHINE HAS SEVERAL VIRTUES. I BELIEVE IT WILL PRINT FASTER THAN I CAN WRITE. ONE MAY LEAN BACK IN HIS CHAIR & WORK IT. IT PILES AN AWFUL STACK OF WORDS ON ONE PAGE. IT DON'T MUSS THINGS OR SCATTER INK BLOTS AROUND.

Sholes and Glidden
typewriter, 1875

It was just before Christmas 1874, and Mark Twain, the famous American author (whose real name was Samuel Langhorne Clemens), had fallen for the first Type-Writer he ever saw.

There it stood in a shop window in Boston. Twain went inside to find out what it was. The salesman explained that this newly invented machine could write at a speed of fifty-seven words a minute. "I don't believe it," Twain said. A young girl was called over to demonstrate the Type-Writer. She dashed off the fifty-seven words in a little under a minute. "That was just luck," said Twain. "Do it again!" As fast as the girl typed, he stuffed the sheets of paper in his pockets for souvenirs. Then he paid a great deal of money, $125, for a machine of his own. When he got back to his hotel, he realized how he had been tricked. The specimens of typing all said the same thing. The girl demonstrator was so fast because she had memorized just one set of words.

When his Remington Model 1 was delivered, the author wrote: "I played with the toy, repeating and repeating and repeating 'The boy stood on the burning deck' until I could turn out that boy's adventure at the rate of twelve words a minute; then I resumed the pen for business, and only worked the machine to astonish inquisitive visitors." In fact, Mark Twain was the first author ever to type out a manuscript (for the book *Life on the Mississippi*) for the publisher.

Columbia typewriter, 1886

The Remington Type-Writer was at first most unsuccessful. Why pay $125 for a writing machine when a pen cost a penny? The public thought that using a typewriter was insulting. "Do you think I can't read?" And they confused this private printing machine with the printing press. Puzzled recipients of early typewritten letters wrote back: "Why did you need to have an ordinary letter to me *printed*?" Yet by 1909 there were a total of eighty-nine typewriter companies in the United States alone. Also on the market were German, Swiss, Italian, French, English and Japanese models.

The typewriter really became popular when it began to be used in offices. At first, salesmen thought that the biggest buyers would be clergymen (for their sermons), writers, and newspapermen. The business world was for men only; offices were gloomy, and sometimes scruffy, places where copy boys sat on high stools, making often inaccurate copies of each hand-written letter before it was posted. Gradually women realized that here was a new career opening up for them. Women had jobs in factories and shops, and worked as domestic servants and cooks. A young lady with some education could only teach or be a nurse. But the typewriter offered a way into the active and interesting world of business. The first batch of girls trained in America to operate the typewriter as a career were snapped up by business houses. Typewriting schools opened all over the country. Suddenly women became office workers. Before, the only women to set foot inside offices had been the cleaners. Business men realized that if they bought a typewriter, they needed a woman to operate it. The typewriter probably did as much to give women freedom and independence as the action of the suffragettes. Of course there were jokes. The operator of a typewriter was called a typewriter too, for at least twenty-five years, until someone thought of the word typist. "What a pretty typewriter you've got there!" People thought it all very funny. But more and more girls were given jobs as typists, and the demand for them seems endless.

Christopher Latham Sholes never made much money from his invention; he sold his share in it before it became popular. He went on inventing typewriters, however, propped up in bed, ill, but unable to stop. Densmore became a typewriter salesman and in the end made his fortune. More inventors than ever began to work on the writing machine after its success, improving it, arguing over different techniques. Lower case (small) letters were added to the typewriter, then the design was altered so that the letters would show as soon as they were typed, instead of being hidden. In a famous victory in 1888 Frank McGurrin beat Louis Traub at a speed-typing contest. He used all ten fingers and the touch type method of never looking at the keys. Portable, and then electric typewriters, were invented. In 1961 the IBM 72 electric typewriter appeared, a revolutionary design with all the letters and symbols (eighty-eight of them) fitted on a revolving metal head about the size of a golf-ball.

The typewriter gave birth to a range of business machines. It is an important part of some computers. The operator uses a typewriter to "tell" the computer what to do, and the computer "replies", also via the typewriter. Children often learn to type at school. Yet of all the machines which are part of our everyday lives, the type-writer is probably one of the most complex and precise. The invention which took over a hundred and fifty years of development before a practical model ever appeared on the market still requires patient hand assembly and skilled adjustment of its two thousand separate parts.

Looking back on it all, Sholes wrote in one of his last letters: "Whatever I may have felt, in the early days, of the value of the typewriter, it is obviously a blessing to man-kind, and especially to womankind. I am glad I have had something to do with it. I builded wiser than I knew, and the world has had the benefit of it."

BALL-POINT PEN

A ball-point pen is often called a Biro, because the brothers Biro invented it.

By the end of the last century several people in different countries had thought of writing with a ball instead of a nib. But none of the methods really worked. Lazlo Biro was a Hungarian sculptor, painter and journalist. His brother Georg was a chemist. They worked on designs for a ball-point pen, and by 1938 applied for patents. Then war came, so the brothers moved to the Argentine and went on with their experiments. Their ball-point pens came on the market during the war and were popular straight away. Here was a new "writing stick" which didn't have a point that broke and needed sharpening like a pencil. And it didn't have a reservoir which needed refilling all the time like a fountain pen. But the ink for ball-points was still a problem because it had to be thick enough not to leak out of the ball, yet dry quickly and cleanly on paper. Fran Seech, an Austrian chemist living in California, invented an ink which greatly improved the ball-point pen. It formed a surface skin as soon as it was exposed to air, and dried instantly. For a while Seech made the ink in his kitchen at home. The first ball-point pens were sold in England for £2.75. Now you can buy throw-away versions at very small cost.

The ball of the pen sits in the metal tip so that it cannot fall out but can roll around easily, collecting ink from the reservoir. Georg Biro thought of putting a tiny vein-like tube between the ball and the reservoir, so that the ball is kept moistened by capillary attraction.

The brothers Biro invented it

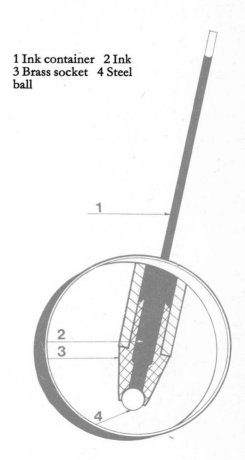

1 Ink container 2 Ink
3 Brass socket 4 Steel ball

THE CHRISTMAS CARD

Post early for Christmas! That advice went out from the Post Office for the first time in 1880

Sir Henry Cole thought up the idea for the first Christmas card in 1843. He could scarcely have imagined into what an enormous industry his idea would grow. Nowadays, the British Post Office handles over eight hundred million Christmas cards a year. Post early for Christmas! That advice went out from the Post Office for the first time in 1880.

Sir Henry Cole asked his friend John Callcott Horsley, a fashionable artist, to design the first Christmas card. Horsley's signature is in the bottom corner, together with a little caricature of himsef. One thousand cards were printed, but they did not sell very well and Sir Henry decided not to repeat the idea next year. Cole was the first director of that great London museum, the Victoria and Albert in South Kensington. He was an energetic man, particularly interested in improving the public's taste, and educating them about art. His Christmas cards were sold in a shop he organized in Bond Street called Felix Summerley's Treasure House. Here children's books with good-quality illustrations were sold, and probably the first ever "Colour Box for Little Painters" with the "10 best colours", brushes, and hints on how to use it all.

The first Christmas card

Some people criticized the Cole and Horsley card because it showed a scene of hearty eating and drinking. Encouraging drunkenness! In fact, Horsley was a very conventional soul; later, because he insisted that artists should not use nude models for their paintings, he was nicknamed Clothes-Horsley.

Cole's card was hand-coloured, artistic and expensive: in 1843 it cost one shilling. Twenty years later the first mass-produced commercial Christmas cards came on the market. They were brightly coloured and cheap; newly developed printing techniques made this possible. The idea of sending Christmas cards really caught on. More of the British public could now read and write. And Sir Rowland Hill's postal reform of 1840 meant it only cost a penny to send one of the new cards, in an envelope, anywhere in the British Isles. Before the reform it cost fourpence to send one sheet of paper fifteen miles, sixpence to send it thirty miles, and an envelope counted as an extra sheet. Letters were usually paid for on delivery, so the postman's visit was not welcome. Now, in the 1860s and 70s, in the middle of Queen Victoria's reign, people began to enjoy sending and receiving Christmas cards. The cards were elaborate and very sentimental, with pictures of cupids, snowy stage-coaches, and little children. They had paper lace stuck around the edges, ribbons, pieces of velvet and glitter. Children and young ladies collected the prettiest Christmas cards and put them into albums to keep alongside mottoes and valentines.

Perhaps the Christmas card grew out of the tradition people in many different countries have had for centuries, a tradition that goes back to the ancient Egyptians and Romans, of exchanging little tokens of friendship at the New Year.

Index